POPULAR COMMUNICATION

Volume 4, Number 3, 2006

At Play: Recent Perspectives From Games Studies

Guest Co-Editors: Katherine Isbister and James Watt

This journal has been abstracted of indexed in *Cambridge Scientific Abstracts: Sociological Abstracts, Family & Society Studies Worldwide, Family Index Database, Linguistics and Language Behavior Abstracts, Social Services Abstracts Worldwide Political Abstracts.*

First published in 2006 by Lawrence Erlbaum Associates, Inc.

This edition published 2014 by Routledge
711 Third Avenue, New York, NY 10017
2 Park Square, Milton Park, Abingdon, Oxon OX14 4RN

Routledge is an imprint of the Taylor & Francis Group, an informa business

POPULAR COMMUNICATION, 4(3), 161–163

At Play: Guest Editors' Introduction

Katherine Isbister and James H. Watt

Rensselaer Polytechnic Institute

Digital games have become a focal point for the popular press in recent years and, increasingly, have become an object of study in the halls of academe. In this special issue, you will find a collection of work that illustrates the wide scope of the intellectual dialogue that has been taking place around digital games. We are delighted to present articles from some of the founders of the game studies area, as well as work from younger researchers who are already making a mark in game studies. One can see from the geographic locations of these contributors (four countries represented in the five articles) that the study of games is a global phenomenon.

Janet Murray of Georgia Institute of Technology, with the publication of her book *Hamlet on the Holodeck* in 1997 and her work since in building the games-related research program in the Department of Literature, Communication, and Culture (where she is Director of Graduate Studies), has been a pioneer of scholarship in this area in the United States. Espen Aarseth is cofounder and Editor-in-Chief of "Game Studies"—one of the primary peer-reviewed journals for game scholarship—and also is Head of Research at one of the premier research foci for game studies, the IT University of Copenhagen. Ian Bogost, a young faculty member at Georgia Institute of Technology, has been building a strong reputation in the area of political games research and development. He is the author of *Unit Operations: An Approach to Videogame Criticism* as well as the forthcoming *Persuasive Games: Videogames and Procedural Rhetoric,* and has been a designer of persuasive games for political organizations. Joost Raessens is a film scholar and Associate Professor of New Media Studies at Utrecht University, The Netherlands. His edited volume, *Handbook for Game Studies,* a comprehensive scholarly treatment of digital games, has just been published by MIT Press. Florence Chee is a Ph.D. Candidate in the School of Communication and Researcher at the Centre for Policy Research on Science and Technology and the Applied Communication and Technology Lab at Simon Fraser University, Vancouver, Canada. Her approach to

Correspondence should be addressed to Katherine Isbister, Department of Language, Literature, and Communication, Rensselaer Polytechnic Institute, 110 8th Street, Troy, NY 12180. E- mail: isbisk@rpi.edu discovering the uses and impact of digital games in a cultural context is an illustration of the breadth of emerging work in understanding digital games in a social and cultural matrix.

Although this special issue focuses on digital games, all contributors are working within the larger conceptual–disciplinary framework of communication. Murray and Bogost are both faculty in Georgia Institute of Technology's Department of Literature, Communication and Culture; Aarseth is a Professor in the Department of Media and Communication in Oslo as well as Head of Research at the Center for Computer Games Research at IT University of Copenhagen; Chee is a graduate student at Simon Fraser University's School of Communication; and Raessens is a faculty member in a department of new media studies at Utrecht University.

The articles in this special issue are situated within some important areas of communication theory and research. Aarseth takes an economic approach to understanding the evolution and role of games in the mix of popular cultural forms that will be valuable to those interested in the impact of media economics and cross-media influence on the development of a new medium. Raessens examines the potential and challenges of games as documentary media, and poses some fundamental questions about the nature of "real" media presentations in a very plastic digital environment. Murray proposes we use evolutionary theory as a lens through which to better understand the role of games in the development of our minds, culture, and language. Bogost brings the analysis of metaphor and thought to an examination of political content and subtext in games in a way that illustrates the emergence of a new and increasingly important form of persuasive interactive media. Chee uses a mixture of empirical strategies to develop a deeper understanding of player social behavior in and around games situated in a particular culture and, thus, illustrates a way to understand this new medium in a popular communication context. Given this range of both theoretical grounding and method of approach, we hope each reader will find something of interest.

ACKNOWLEDGMENTS

Our thanks to Sharon Mazzarella and Norma Pecora for inviting us to bring this special issue together, and many thanks to all of the authors for their thoughtful and timely contributions.

Katherine Isbister is an Associate Professor in the Department of Language, Literature and Communication at Rensselaer Polytechnic Institute, and an Associate of the Rensselaer Social and Behavioral Research Laboratory. She founded the Games Research Lab at Rensselaer in 2004, where she studies social and emotional aspects of digital game design. She is the author of Better Game Characters by Design: A Psychological Approach, to be released by Morgan Kaufmann in 2006.

James Watt is Director of the Rensselaer Social and Behavioral Research Laboratory and Professor of Communication in the Department of Language, Literature, and Communication. He is Chair of the Game Studies SIG of the International Communication Association and has been active in defining a new B.S. degree in Games and Simulation Arts and Sciences, to be offered by Rensselaer in Fall, 2006.

POPULAR COMMUNICATION, 4(3), 165–183

Videogames and Ideological Frames

Ian Bogost

The Georgia Institute of Technology

Based on cognitive linguist George Lakoff's notions of metaphor and frame as the principle organizers of political discourse, this article offers an approach to analyzing political rhetoric in videogames intended to carry ideological bias. I then argue for 3 ways games function in relation to ideological frames—reinforcement, contestation, and exposition—through examples of political games (*Tax Invaders*), art games (*Vigilance 1.0*), and commercial games (*Grand Theft Auto: San Andreas*). I also offer thoughts on issues likely to arise from the hypothetical adoption of political frame and metaphor as design principles.

The 2004 U.S. presidential election renewed world citizens' recognition of an ideological polarization in U.S. politics. The American electoral college, combined with the lack of a viable third-party, only increased the apparent split. Massive, telecast electoral college maps displaying won states in red (Republican) and blue (Democrat) suggested a geographic divide to many Americans, with the west coast, northeast, and Great Lakes areas voting Democratic and the heartland and south Republican. Yet more detailed maps that showed county-by-county vote balance proved that the division runs even deeper (Vanderbei, 2004), with most counties appearing some shade of purple, a combination of "red votes" and "blue votes." In the aftermath of the election, Democrats acknowledged that their messages failed, just as Republicans recognized how much theirs succeeded. Juxtaposing American morality against British class rifts, some cite religion as the key issue dividing the presidential vote (Schifferes, 2004a). The left is now scrambling to develop a new strategy. Ideas are plentiful: Avoid candidates from the northeast (Wallsten & Anderson, 2004), focus more strongly on domestic issues (Schifferes, 2004b), and seek better management (Marinucci, 2004). But two influential political theorists and cognitive linguists suggested that such superficial strategies will

Correspondence should be addressed to Ian Bogost, The Georgia Institute of Technology, School of Literature Communication and Culture, 686 Cherry Street, Atlanta, GA 30332. E-mail: ian.bogost@lcc.gatech.edu not move the political needle; instead, political success draws less from reality and more from representation.

Lakoff (1990) and Lakoff and Johnson (1980) suggested that metaphor is central to human understanding. Lakoff and Johnson (influenced by Levi-Strauss, Clifford Geertz, and Jean Piaget) argued that our conceptual systems are fundamentally shaped by cultural constructions. For Lakoff and Johnson, metaphor is not a fanciful language reserved for poets, but an active framework central to how we understand the world. For example, the two unpack our understanding of time as a commodity, showing how we relate our experience of time to monetary concepts of quantification (you are running out of time; is that worth the time?). Turning to politics explicitly, Lakoff (1996) argued that the most important consideration in political discourse is not how politicians respond to the "facts" of the external world, but how they conceptualize, or "frame" that world in their discourse about it. Lakoff argued that political frames in the contemporary United States reflect metaphors of family management—conservatives frame political issues as "strict fathers," whereas liberals frame them as "nurturing parents" (p. 63). A self-professed liberal, Lakoff (2004) argued that if the left wants to regain political credibility, they need to start crafting their political speech with an understanding of liberal and conservative frames. They need to create words that reflect their ideas.

On the other side of the political fence, conservative political scientist Frank Luntz (2003) specializes in helping conservatives frame their spoken discourse to create the greatest appeal possible—what he called "message development" (pp. 131–135). Luntz was responsible for much of Newt Gingrich's 1994 "Contract for America," and more recently he guided conservatives on the strategic use of such terms as "war on terror" instead of "war in Iraq" and "climate change" instead of "global warming." What Lakoff called "frames," Luntz (2002, 2004) named "contexts"—ways to repackage positions so they carry more political currency.

Some have criticized Luntz's (2002, 2004) message development strategy as misleading or even immoral. The National Environmental Trust (2003) maintains www.luntzspeak.com, a Web site devoted to exposing and critiquing the Luntz messaging strategy. Despite such criticism, politicians have taken Luntz's advice to heart, and evidence of his influence and success are increasingly apparent. At the 1998 unveiling of the Council of Republicans for Environmental Advocacy, founder Gale A. Norton argued that public lands should support "multiple use," a Luntz-influenced context meant to suggest that such lands might be used for their resources in addition to being protected for wildlife (Booth, 2001). In 2001, the Interior Department passed a policy allowing local authorities the ability to exercise right of way for roads across federal lands (Cart, 2003). The policy did not automatically allow local municipalities to bulldoze and pave remote country, but it did recontextualize public lands as areas in which commercial activity might have a future place. Frames or contexts are not merely theoretical structures for intellectual navel gazing; they are operational models that are actively influencing public policy.

POLITICAL VIDEOGAMES

There are many precedents for commercial games that carry political messages. Well-known designer and video game pundit Chris Crawford's (1985) classic *Balance of Power* is often cited as the first political game in which diplomacy outweighed brute force. In the game, the player uses treaties; diplomacy; international espionage; and, as a last resort, military force to manage a world in the throes of the cold war. In an early example of game-based political expression, Crawford imbued his own worldview into the game play. Inciting a nuclear war caused a most grave lose condition in the game—a black screen imprinted with plain white offering a dour report of the player's outcome, "You have ignited a nuclear war. And no, there is no animated display or a mushroom cloud with parts of bodies flying through the air. We do not reward failure." Larry Barbu's (1991) cold war sim *Crisis in the Kremlin* followed in the tradition of *Balance of Power,* challenging the player to stay in power and to prevent the Soviet Union from dismantling. In 1990 two games were created that explored environmental issues. The first and more well-known was Maxis's (1990) *Sim Earth: The Living Planet,* a game adaptation of James Lovelock's Gaia Hypothesis—the theory that the earth functions as a continuous system for all life rather than a vessel for specific forms of life. In *Sim Earth*, the player nurtures single-cell organisms into capable complex organisms with intelligence enough to leave the planet. Pollution, disease, and global warming are among the obstacles that stand in the way. The second, more obscure environmental game of 1990 was Chris Crawford's (1990) environmental follow-up to *Balance of Power,* called *Balance of the Planet,* and it was released that year on the first celebration of Earth Day. The game offered a model of the earth's ecosystem, and a much more detailed one than *Sim Earth.* Crawford constructed some 200 individual environment factors such as lung disease, coal use, and coal tax—all of which were interconnected in a complex chain of causes and effects. Instead of manipulating the physical environment itself, as in *Sim Earth*, in *Balance of the Planet* the player manipulates social response to environmental conditions. For example, lowering the coal tax increases coal use, which in turn increases lung disease caused by coal pollution. In addition to changing environmental incentives, Crawford also allows the player to adjust the formula inputs used to calculate the results themselves. For example, a player can ratchet down the effect of coal-burning energy on lung cancer, effectively reducing the coupling between that particular cause and effect.

In addition to these early examples of politically charged commercial games, increasingly larger numbers of independently created games about political issues have cropped up on the Internet. Gonzalo Frasca (2003) launched www.newsgaming.com, a Web site to host games about current events. Frasca called newsgames a merger of video games and political cartoons and offered a first example of such a one, *September 12*. The reader is referred to my lengthy discussion of the game elsewhere (Bogost, 2006), but the general theme of *September 12* is noteworthy for its unabashed bias. In the game, the player controls a missile crosshairs aimed at an anonymous middle-eastern town. Both innocent citizens and terrorists scurry around the town, and the player is faced with the problem of what to do about the terrorists. Although the latter effect no actual terrorist activity during game play, their threat is implied. If the player chooses to fire missiles, after a small launch delay a huge explosion destroys the area underneath the crosshair, and also a great deal of the surrounding area, including any people unfortunate enough to have been in the vicinity. When the player's missiles kill innocents, nearby citizens crowd around and mourn over the bodies before turning into terrorists themselves. The game's rules enforce a particular perspective: Violence begets more violence, and the nonprecision weapons of American "precision warfare" bear significant consequence in the form of innocent lives lost. Another pacifist game released in the aftermath of the September 11th terror attacks was *Antiwargame* (On, 2001), created by former Ars Electronica Golden Nica winner Josh On and his artist collective Futurefarmers. *Antiwargame* offers a simulation dynamic depicting the bind between homeland politics and foreign war.

These precedents are but a few of the previous commercial and independent games that have addressed political problems. But a major shift in the subgenre of political video games took place in 2004. In addition to becoming the year of an American political divide, 2004 was also the year when political video games became legitimate. For the first time, candidates and party groups created officially endorsed games to bolster their campaign for U.S. President (Bogost & Frasca, 2003; Republican National Committee, 2004), U.S. State Legislature (Bogost, 2004b), U.S. Congress (Bogost, 2004a), and even President of Uruguay (Frasca, 2004). As the worlds of political message strategy and political videogames gain momentum, an opportunity arises for each to inform the other. As videogames become a part of endorsed political speech, they will become more tightly integrated with existing strategies for political discourse.

But Frank Luntz's (2002) contextual message development and George Lakoff's (1990, 1996) framed conceptual systems both define strategies for *spoken or written* political rhetoric. As such, these methods may be inappropriate for videogames, in which the main representational mode is procedural rather than verbal. The remainder of this article offers an approach to analyzing political rhetoric in videogames intended to carry ideological bias, paying special attention to the work of framing as a procedural rather than verbal strategy. I argue for three ways games function in relation to ideological frames—reinforcement, contestation, and exposition—through examples of art games, political games, and commercial games.

REINFORCEMENT

Customary uses of language do have some place in videogame based political messaging. The GOP's second game of the 2004 campaign, *Tax Invaders* (Republican National Committee, 2004), is a replica of the classic arcade game *Space Invaders* (Taito, 1978), but players defend the country against John Kerry's tax plans instead of a swarm of descending aliens. The player controls the disembodied head of George W. Bush, which he or she moves from side to side along the bottom of the screen in place of the original game's space gun. The player combats potential John Kerry tax cuts, represented as abstract rectangles bearing the numerical value of the proposed tax. The player fires projectiles out of the top of Bush's head to "shoot down" the tax hikes and defend the country.

The game's implementation is extremely crude—so crude that when I first played it, I quickly dismissed its rhetorical power, assuming it to be as rudimentary as the game's primitive visual and programmatic execution. If left long enough, the taxes–aliens pass over the player and off the bottom of the screen. And the blue "shields"—a critical strategic tool in *Space Invaders*—are rendered impotent in *Tax Invaders*. They seem to have been placed merely for show, or perhaps the game's programmers did not have time to turn them into active protective barriers. The game play itself amounts to a three-level long barrage of counter-tax projectiles. But since this original experience I have revisited the game, and I am now convinced that it represents one of the most sophisticated examples of a rhetorical frame at work, not just in videogame form, but anywhere in contemporary political discourse.

Within the game, written text contextualizes the player's actions. The copywriting enacts logic familiar to both Lakoff (1996) and Luntz (2002): It casts tax increases as an anthropomorphized enemy in itself—a thief against whom you must defend yourself. The game's opening text announces, "Only *you* can stop the tax invader," and it invites the player to "Save the USA from John Kerry's tax ideas." Lakoff argued that such language reflects an underlying logic at work in conservative politics— that citizens know what is best for themselves and that material success is moral and should not be punished. Conservatives, he suggested, conceptualize theft as a metaphor for taxation. The language that literally frames the game conforms to this metaphor; the player is contextualized as a force of good, "stopping" taxes and "saving" the country from them. *Tax Invaders* extends the verbal metaphor of "taxation as theft" to the tangible plane.

Released in March 2004 at the height of the second Gulf War, some might find it surprising that the GOP would choose to publish a depiction of George W. Bush shooting anything. But within the verbal rhetoric of conservative politics, taxation is a "battle" to be waged. Lakoff argued that, from the conservative perspective, tax increases are never proposals to improve the general social good, but always threats on the part of the government to steal what does not rightly belong to them. When someone breaks into your home, it is appropriate to brandish a gun. It is your property and you have to defend it. There is thus no political inconsistency in contextualizing tax opposition as hostility; indeed as violent hostility. In the context of *Tax Invaders*, George W. Bush's bullet-like projectiles are not akin to Army rifles wielded against innocent Iraqis, but rather to the policeman's sidearm wielded against a criminal.

A simple game such as *Tax Invaders* could be said to wear its rhetorical frame on its sleeve; indeed, the instantiations of conservative contexts are almost identical to their verbal counterparts. For example, we talk about politicians "shooting down" a measure in Congress. This figure even seems to function outside of the English language. In the aftermath of Hurricane Katrina in early autumn 2005, a German social minister used this verbal figure to attach President George W. Bush's handling of the crisis in New Orleans: "He ought to be shot down [gehört abgeschossen]." He later clarified that he meant the statement "in the political sense" (Reuters, 2005). The idea of a legislator "shooting down" a tax hike proposal is thus extremely plausible; the game just makes such a verbal frame materially manifest.

But *Tax Invaders* takes the metaphor beyond even visual rhetoric. One could imagine a political cartoon that literalized the verbal metaphor of legislation as battle. One side might throw out proposals for new laws or candidates for official posts that the opposing side would view as assaults rather than propositions, on which they would then open fire. Such a cartoon might effectively illustrate one party's unwillingness to consider the other's potentially legitimate proposals, for example. Such a cartoon would illustrate the verbal metaphor, rendering that metaphor into its visual equivalent. *Tax Invaders* frames the metaphors of its rhetoric even further—as embodied activities. Bush (and by extension the player) fires projectiles at the tax cuts, representing the metaphor of tax hikes as enemy threat. No matter the player's political perspective. To play the game at all he or she must step inside the skin of the taxation opponent, viewing taxes as a foreign enemy—in this case the most foreign enemy, a wholly other enemy whose very name means "otherness" itself: the alien.

Thus although *Tax Invaders* does little to represent actual tax policy, it frames tax policy in a way that reinforces a conservative position. The short text descriptions that bracket the game do bear a striking resemblance to verbal rhetoric used elsewhere in conservative politics. That resemblance should come as no surprise, because experienced conservative communication personnel probably penned the lines. But this verbal language remains largely imperceptible to the player; its function as metaphor is hidden to a public mired in their own familiarity with those metaphors. More surprising is the game's remarkable translation of the frame of taxation as theft from verbal to procedural form. The GOP authors of the game may not have had such a high-minded goal as to adapt their Luntz-style verbal rhetoric into computer code. Instead they likely took advantage of the resonance between this particular verbal metaphor and an existing, well-seated videogame mechanic (firing projectiles at things). Better yet, the GOP was able to find an existing game with a suitable, adaptable mechanic and, better still, a game with tremendous cultural currency, such that its constituency would find the game immediately approachable. After all, *Space Invaders* was first released in 1978, making it a good fit for voters in their 40s and 50s who would remember playing the game in arcades, as well as younger voters who could not have escaped *Space Invaders'* cultural wake.

George Lakoff (1996) argued that the conservative worldview holds the wealthy up as model citizens because they have worked hard and achieved success at their own hands, rather than from relying on tax-funded social programs. Conservatives view taxation as punishment, and in Lakoff's words, "that makes the federal government a thief" (p. 189). The political right views liberals' inclination to think of taxes as civic duty or even payment for government services as misguided: In the case of civic duty, conservatives see no obligation to contribute to the general assistance of the citizenry as a matter of principle. In the case of payment for services, conservatives point out that citizens do not have a choice to "purchase" the services funded by tax dollars. And furthermore, conservatives suggest that the government has a bad reputation for running ragged, primarily because it has no profit motive to drive efficient management, as would a business. Lakoff convincingly showed that opposition to taxation is fundamental to conservative politics because it underwrites so many other conservative positions. This includes things such as the drive to privatize government, turning poorly run federal and local services into well-run businesses with profit motives; the drive to reduce or eliminate social services in favor of strengthening backbone and enforcing personal responsibility as the primary factor in a thriving citizenry; the belief that people are fundamentally driven by reward and punishment; and taking away hard-earned cash from personally responsible citizens to give it to the irresponsible stinks of injustice.

Tax Invaders is an example of the reinforcement of an ideological frame. Typical political discourse would invoke the metaphor of taxation as theft or legislation as battle through verbal or written speech. For example, a politician might vow to "strike down new tax proposals" or warn that he or she might "return dollars stolen from Americans through unjust taxes." But *Tax Invaders* draws attention to the correlation between war and taxation, taxation and enemy threat, and taxation and theft. As a matter of cultural practice, alien invasions are tightly tied to theft. Alien abduction in the vein of *The X-Files* (Carter, 1993) is perhaps the best example, but alien invasions from *The War of the Worlds* (Wells, 1898) to *Independence Day*

(Emmerich, 1996) all depict the aliens as malevolent agents bent on stealing the very planet Earth from its inhabitants. There is perhaps no more effective metaphor for theft than alien invasion.

Verbal or written rhetoric relies on our intrinsic experiences with metaphor as fluent speakers of a language. When listening to a politician on the soapbox, most of us would not even make note of the metaphors of theft and battle. The insight and utility of Lakoff's (1996) work on metaphor spoke to the ideology of the spoken word: Its logic must be exposed as a platform for the way we think, because it is not immediately obvious that conceptual metaphor underlies what we say and write. *Tax Invaders* not only makes its argument from within the conservative frame on taxation, but also it explicitly draws attention to the frame itself. The rules of the game—aliens descend continuously, the player character combats them before they reach the bottom—stand as symbolic structures of a higher order than natural language. These procedural metaphors operationalize the figures of the verbal metaphor into a functional system whose very function represents the desired position. Here the battle is both metaphoric and material. The player actually does battle against taxes, in a literal sense. I have called the general, procedural representation of abstract concepts *unit operations* (Bogost, 2006). *Tax Invaders* presents a set of unit operations for the conservative frame on taxation itself. Whereas verbal rhetoric invokes the frame (or context, to use Luntz's word) without acknowledging that the frame even exists, let alone structures the rhetoric, procedural rhetoric depicts the frame itself in a tangible form. *Tax Invaders* offers an unusual view onto the conservative frame for tax policy itself. In playing the game, the player is encouraged not only to consider and reaffirm a conservative position on taxation, but also to consider and practice using a conservative frame for that position.

A game such as *Tax Invaders* can thus serve opposing political purposes. For conservatives it reinforces the notion that taxes are an invasion and we need to "wage war" against them, as we would against alien invaders. This sort of rhetoric would be much more difficult, or at least more inappropriate, to enact on the soapbox. On the public pulpit, grandstanding politicians rely on the perlocutionary rather than illocutionary effect of their rhetorical frame. In speech act theory, an illocutionary act carries propositional content that the utterance expresses literally. A perlocutionary act carries an effect that is not expressed in the utterance, such as persuasion (Austin, 1962; Searle, 1969). *Tax Invaders* offers the unique ability to convert perlocution into illocution. Instead of using verbal frames, the GOP has made the symbolic underpinning of their rhetorical context manifest in the game rules itself: a procedural rather than a verbal rhetoric. In essence, *Tax Invaders* is a lesson in how to think about tax policy as a conservative would. The game says, "Think of taxation as an invasion meant to harm you" rather than saying, "We must fight against tax increases." For liberals, *Tax Invaders* reinforces the conservative frame on taxation, forcing such players to enact the conservative position that taxation is a theft rather than a contribution to the common social good. Playing the game critically might assist liberals in orienting their frame in opposition to that of conservatives. The game's crudeness only underscores how foundational the metaphor of taxation as theft is for conservative politics and, therefore, how challenging opposition to it may prove. Each perspective is one side of the same coin. Although *Tax Invaders* offers only a very rudimentary treatment of tax policy, it offers a more sophisticated reinforcement of a conservative rhetorical frame on tax policy.

CONTESTATION

Tax Invaders mounts its argument partly from the verbal register (the text inside the game) and partly through macroscopic imagery (George W. Bush as hero and the descending taxes). Although it does depict the rules that constitute the conservative frame on taxation, it borrows those rules entirely from another videogame. To further understand the way frames and ideological bias function in videogames, we must look at how the interactions of new rules create similar frames as verbal political rhetoric.

In French artist Martin Le Chevallier's (2000) installation game *Vigilance 1.0,* players seek out deviants on surveillance screen-like sections of an urban environment. The game screen is divided into small squares, each of which displays a different segment and scale of the detailed city. Citizens traverse the environment, executing tasks typical of everyday urban life, such as shopping at the supermarket or relaxing in a park. The player's task is to watch these screens and identify improprieties ranging from littering to vagrancy to prostitution. Armed with a small circular cursor, the player must constantly scan the environment, pointing out infractions by clicking on offenders. For each success, the player is rewarded with points proportional to the severity of the offense (e.g., littering is valued at 1 point and prostitution at 5). Erroneous identifications cost the player points for "defamation." The game is programmed to increase or decrease social problems in proportion with the player's success at responding to them. With every offender that passes by unnoticed, the more depraved the society becomes, and vice versa.

Vigilance's rules are incredibly simple. The player can censure citizens; successes are rewarded and failures punished; and for each success the society becomes more pure, whereas for each failure or omission more base. It is a game about surveillance disguised as one about moral depravity, the 16 rectangular segments of the screen akin to a security guard's video monitors. The player's "vigilance" quickly devolves into its own perversion—that of unfettered surveillance.

Because the game creates a positive feedback loop for depravity in the society, any attempt on the player's part to cease his or her vigilant oversight creates more corruption, reinforcing the need to monitor. By forcing the player to see the consequences of the metaphor of vigilance as comprehensive regulation, the game challenges the ideological frame it initially represents. The game's purpose is not to promote surveillance nor moral purity, but to call such values into question by turning the apparently upstanding player into one of the depraved whom he or she is charged to eliminate.

On first blush, the game seems to reinforce the ideological frame of vigilance as safeguard. The game supports this sentiment through its rules, which provide positive feedback for increased surveillance. But over time, the player comes to realize that his or her adopted role as overseer is no less perverse than the game's abstract representations of moral depravity—prostitution, vagrancy, and zoophilia. The game then affords the player a variety of ways to interrogate this challenge.

The game's reinforcement system encourages players to calculate one offense in terms of another: five litterbugs for every prostitute. The notion of equivalence between actions and their consequences evokes another metaphor for political thought—what Lakoff (1996) called keeping the moral books. In Lakoff's view, we conceptualize well-being as wealth. Changes to our well-being are thus akin to gains and losses. Lakoff characterized this metaphorical understanding of morality in terms of financial transactions. Individuals and societies alike have "moral debts" and "moral credits" that must sum to zero. Moral accounting implies the need for reciprocation and retribution; good actions must be rewarded, and harmful ones must be punished. That punishment might include restitution, which can in turn take many forms, from contrition to prison. When we speak of criminals who have completed their sentences, we often say that they have paid their debt to society. In a moral system of this type, "the moral books must be balanced" (Lakoff, 1996, p. 46).

In contemporary U.S. politics, a fair society is generally conceived as one in which an authority keeps track of the moral books and does the moral accounting. This metaphorical Chief Financial Officer takes many forms, from the courts to the police to the parent at the cookie jar. Lakoff (1996) identified one common attitude toward public justice that stems directly from the concept of moral accounting. He called this model "procedural fairness" or "the impartial rule-based distribution of opportunities to participate, talk, state one's case, and so on" (p. 61). Here the term "procedural" refers to the invocation of legal rules that determine what behavior is allowed and prohibited in a society.

In one version of procedural fairness, the failure to account for improprieties puts the books out of balance. *Vigilance* allows the player to experiment within this frame. The game deploys an arithmetic algorithm to control the amount of depravity to feed back into the system. Identifying more perverse acts increases the score more rapidly. For example, public drunkenness is worth 2 points and abandoned trash 1 point. The player could choose to target only the most egregious acts as a kind of strategy for more efficient moral sanctity. But while watching for public urination or prostitution, many more low-level acts will already have begun to cause the society to spiral into further chaos. The frequency of low-level acts is higher, giving players an opportunity to locate and identify more litterbugs and drunkards for every prostitute, public urinator, or pedophile.

At the same time, the game forces the player to recognize the consequence of blind moral accounting. When one pedophile equals three drunkards equals six litterbugs, both the acts and the contexts for those acts are occluded. As Lakoff (1996) pointed out, "rule-based fairness invites dispute over how impartial the rules really are" (p. 61). When the player of *Vigilance* clicks indiscriminately on vagrants and violent criminals alike, he or she is forced to think of each as a variety of the same, underlying moral depravity. The game does not afford the player the ability to consider the impartiality of the rules of surveillance and, thus, invites reflection on the nature of each particular act. Why is the drunkard drunk? Is he or she unaware of social convention? Is he or she mentally ill and in need of assistance? Has he or she suffered a personal tragedy and is calling out for empathy?

I argued previously that simulations exist in the gap between rule-based representations and a user's subjectivity (Bogost, 2006). *Vigilance* thus provides a variety of player-configurable lenses through which to consider and reconsider the ideological frame of vigilance as inviolability. As the player identifies more and more deviants, Le Chevallier (2000) intended the game to slowly but progressively change the focus from balancing the society's moral books to questioning procedural fairness as a legitimate strategy for running a society. Most explicitly, *Vigilance* attempts to identify such moral bookkeeping as a disturbing panopticon. But the game also challenges other aspects of the frame of justice as balanced moral books: moral depravation and criminality as a slippery slope of interrelated behaviors, and social justice as removal or incarceration rather than social support and reformation.

IMPLICATION

Both *Vigilance 1.0* and *Tax Invaders* could be seen as special cases—games created explicitly with ideological bias in mind (one for artistic reasons and one for political reasons). Commercial games may be less deliberate in their rhetoric, but they are not necessarily free from ideological framing. Such games may imply complex procedural rhetoric with or without the conscious intention of the designers. Although the rhetorical intentions of the GOP or artists such as Le Chevallier (2000) are palpable, the relative obscurity of those games restricts their influence. But procedural rhetoric in commercial games—the most successful of which easily sell between 5 and 10 million copies—trade forthrightness for authority. And that authority can occlude the ideological frames popular commercial games operationalize, rendering them implicit and in need of critique.

In *Grand Theft Auto: San Andreas* (Rockstar Games, 2004), players enact the life of an early 1990s Los Angeles "gangbanger." Whereas previous iterations of the series favored stylized representations of historico-fictional times and places (Rockstar Games, 2001, 2003), *San Andreas* takes on a cultural moment steeped in racial and economic politics. Rather than taking on the role of an organized criminal, the player is cast as CJ, an inner-city gangster. *Grand Theft Auto's* use of large navigable spaces and open-ended game play have been widely cited and praised, but in *San Andreas* open game play, expansive virtual spaces, and the inner-city characterization collide to underscore opportunity biases.

San Andreas added the requirement that CJ eat to maintain his stamina and strength. However, the only nourishment in the game comes from fast food restaurants (chicken, burgers, or pizza). Eating moderately maintains energy, but eating high fat content foods increases CJ's weight, and fat gangsters cannot run or fight very effectively. Each food item in the game comes at a cost, and the player's funds are limited. Mirroring real fast food restaurants, less fattening foods such as salad cost more than high-calorie super meals. The dietary features of *San Andreas* are rudimentary, but the fact that the player must feed his or her character to continue playing does draw attention to the material conditions the game provides for satisfying that need. This subtly exposes the fact that problems of obesity and malnutrition in poor communities can partly be attributed to the relative ease and affordability of fast food.

Evidence has suggested that citizens on fixed incomes, such as students and the working poor, have easiest access to fast food, and as a result of this convenience they eat more of it. Fast food has even penetrated our very health care infrastructure. More than one third of top U.S. hospitals have a fast food outlet on premises (Markel, 2003). Nutritionist Marion Nestle (2002) devoted much of her career to identifying the relation between nutrition, food policy, and food industry marketing. Obesity, argued Nestle, replaced dietary insufficiency as the major nutritional problem in the United States in the 100 years since the turn of the 19th century (Nestle, 2002). Nestle traced the connections between obesity and a food industry intent on increasing food consumption to drive profits. One major contributor to the problem is portion size. According to Nestle, Americans consume larger portions of over one third of all foods, including bread, french fries, and soft drinks. The familiar "super size" fast food option is one example, immortalized in Morgan Spurlock's (2004) Oscar-nominated documentary *Super Size Me*. Today, Americans worry about avian flu and chemical weapons attacks, but we also stuff ourselves with high-sugar Krispy Kremes; cholesterol-raising hydrogenated oils; and high-fat, low-nutrient foods. Fad diets such as Atkins focus on quick results at the cost of long-term health. Nestle and Spurlock's work underscored the same basic principle: Obesity and other threats to public health are at best encouraged, and at worst directly caused by the food market itself.

The tension between personal responsibility and social forces is related to another of Lakoff's (1996) metaphors for political thought—what he called "moral strength" (p. 74). Moral strength entails the courage to stand up to both internal and external evils, and it is fundamentally related to will. In Lakoff's model, moral strength comes from self-discipline and self-denial. The disciplined person is strong, and therefore moral, whereas the man who cannot stand up to temptation is weak, and therefore immoral. Lakoff explicitly linked moral strength with asceticism. Self-indulgence and "moral flabbiness" are the domain of the morally weak (p. 74). Moral strength is fundamentally a conservative political frame that stands in contrast to the liberal equivalents of empathy and nurturance (Lakoff, 1996).

It is no accident that flabbiness would come up in a discussion of moral strength. In the conservative frame, obesity and poor health are tied to self-control or the ability to assess and resist the internal temptation to eat the wrong food, or to overeat. In such a worldview, a problem such as obesity has nothing to do with the food industry Nestle (2002) and Spurlock (2004) renounced. The executives at fast food corporations and the proprietors of their franchises are fulfilling another aspect of conservative moral strength. Businesspeople are morally strong agents with self-discipline enough to work hard and earn material success (Lakoff, 1996). The apparent conflict between the morally strong entrepreneur and the morally weak overeater are not contradictory for conservatives. The latter are conceived as lesser citizens by the morally strong conservative, and gaining material advantage at their expense only further underscores both the moral and material superiority of the former. In Lakoff's own words, the conservative frame of moral strength "rules out any explanations in terms of social forces or social class" (p. 75).

That fast food restaurants represent the only path to sustenance in *Grand Theft Auto: San Andreas,* and that such sustenance is required to progress and achieve goals in the game suggests two possible interpretations. On the one hand, the fact that food comes only from fast food joints implies a social condition more like the critique Nestle (2002), Spurlock (2004), and others have mounted against the fast food and packaged foods industries. For the less-fortunate in particular, the cheap, factory-style, high-fat, low-nutrient food of the burger joint or taco hut represents the easiest and most viable way to fill a grumbling stomach. When these establishments try to provide more healthful meals, such as salads, they come at a cost premium. As I write this in late 2005, a "premium salad" at McDonalds costs $4.99, whereas a Big Mac costs $2.59.[1] Under this interpretation, *San Andreas's* enforcement of fast food eating serves to expose the social forces that drive the poor and working-class residents of the inner-city to consume fast food habitually. The game even allows the player to reap the health detriments of a fast food diet in the form of lost stamina and lost respect (see the following for more on this point).

---

[1]The salad, when eaten with the dressing it comes with, totals nearly as many calories as a Big Mac. Some configurations of the salad with dressing even offer more grams of total fat than a Big Mac. See http://www.mcdonalds.com/app_controller.nutrition.index1.html

Even if the player does not play enough (or eat enough) to make CJ turn from a lithe youth into a portly one, the game's insistence that the player eat only at fast food restaurants draws attention to the social reality of poverty and its related health effects. Players of *San Andreas* might leave the game and make new observations about the world around them, and how social opportunity and disclosure often overshadows the issue of self-restraint.

On the other hand, the game seems to allow the player to overcome the social conditions of poverty and poor nutrition through hard work—a textbook example of moral strength. No matter what the player eats in the pizza place or the chicken hut, he or she can always build a ripped chest and six-pack for CJ by working out constantly in the game's gym. Furthermore, the more "healthful" salad meals at the restaurants cost more money, and the player earns money primarily through the "work" of playing the game. To be fair, that work is almost exclusively limited to violent crime, a topic that I return to shortly. Despite its apparent support for nutrition as a condition of social station, *San Andreas* allows the player to overcome that condition through relatively simple, if sometimes tedious, work and exercise. Such rules might tilt the game toward a more conservative frame—one in which discipline and hard work can overcome material conditions.

The game's use of open-ended virtual spaces presents a less ambiguous frame for social class, race, and criminality. *San Andreas* intricately recreates representations of three huge cities (the equivalents of Los Angeles; San Francisco; and Las Vegas, NV) along with rural spaces in between. CJ has recently returned to his hometown neighborhood (the *San Andreas* equivalent of Compton in Los Angeles) to avenge his mother's death. The player can customize CJ's clothes to some extent and, of course, steal nice cars for him, but he remains a Black youth from Compton wearing gang-associated paraphernalia. Thanks to the immense simulated space of the city, the player can travel from neighborhood to neighborhood, and the buildings, scenery, vehicles, and people adjust accordingly. But something remains the same everywhere in *San Andreas,* from its Compton to its Beverly Hills: No matter the location, the game's non-player characters respond to your semiautomatic-toting, do-rag wearing Black "gangsta" character in roughly the same way.

Although major technology challenges impede the development of credible character interactions in an environment as large-scale as San Andreas and its surrounds (see Mateas & Stern, 2002), the game makes no effort to alter character behavior based on race, social standing, or location. Bumping into a leggy blonde on the equivalent of Beverly Hills' Rodeo Drive elicits the same anonymous outcry as would jostling a drug dealer on Compton's Atlantic Drive. When mediated by the game's inner-city context, its procedural interaction of space and character creates a frame in which the player's street gang persona does not participate in any historical, economic, racial, or social disadvantage. The aggregate procedural effects in *San Andreas* thus expose an ideological frame, and perhaps a surprising one.

Lakoff (1996) argued that the conservative frame for crime is an extension of the "strict father" model of seeing the world. The strict father disciplines his children and acts as a moral authority. Through this example, he instills discipline and self-reliance. Self-reliant, morally disciplined adults make the right decisions and prosper. Morally depraved adults do not deserve to prosper and may even be dangerous. Lakoff contrasted the conservative strict father with the progressive "nurturing parent." Unlike the strict father, the nurturing parent believes that support and assistance helps people thrive, and that people who need help deserve to be helped. Nurturing parents reject self-discipline as the sole justification of prosperity and allow for economic, cultural, or social disadvantages that might suggest some people deserve even more assistance.

By avoiding interactions across the socioeconomic boundaries of the game's virtual space, *San Andreas* is implicated in a logic similar to the conservative frame on crime. If the non-player character's logic were to admit to cultural and economic disadvantages as factors that mediate interaction between characters, it would also have to admit that such factors are external to CJ (the player's character) and thus attributable to something outside CJ's character and self-discipline. As in the case of nutrition, from a frame of moral strength CJ's criminal behavior can be explained only by a lack of self-control and self-discipline. Any morally upstanding young man would find a legitimate job and earn his way off the street without resorting to criminality. But interestingly, the game turns this frame in on itself. To succeed in the mission-based story of *San Andreas*, the player effectively builds a sizable, if illegitimate, business of thug activities, based on a staple of drive-by shootings and armed robbery. Yet the game is a veritable rags-to-riches story. As the game starts, CJ is returning to Los Santos from Liberty City (the home city of *Grand Theft Auto III*), where he had fled the gang-ridden streets of his youth, presumably as a reformed man. He returns only to bury his mother, another victim of gang violence, and gets caught up in reclaiming his old neighborhood from the rival gangs who are dismantling it. As CJ, the player must build "respect" between both his or her own gang members and rival gang members, eventually earning their trust and constructing an ever-larger gang of followers.

The addition of respect signals an unusual perversion of the traditional, conservative concept of moral authority. On the one hand, CJ's life on the street bears a striking resemblance to that of the political conservative. He takes responsibility for his family and takes it on himself to build a new life of material wealth and personal safety. His authority demands respect from others, and those whose respect he demands stand subordinate to him. His own personal self-discipline even contributes to this respect. A well-padded CJ who eats too many burgers and does not work out earns less respect than a muscle-ripped CJ. On the other hand, CJ earns such respect entirely through felonious behavior. He acts with a similar underlying value structure as the ideal conservative, but uses lawless rather than lawful material production as his medium. This inversion of the typical conservative frame could be read as a satire—the very same rules of behavior produce a very different outcome.

But outside of the game's tightly woven mission-based story line, *Grand Theft Auto: San Andreas* implies clear support for the metaphor of crime as decadence. Despite its purported open-endedness, *San Andreas* offers incentives to play its missions, and thus incentives to engage in criminal behavior. Although the story does question whether gang members have legitimate moral options—at the start of the game CJ is set up by a corrupt cop and sent on the run—once outside of the mission architecture, the game has no procedure in place to mediate character interactions. Notably, the open-ended game play reorients the player back toward the missions. The game will not unlock areas beyond Los Santos unless the player reaches key points in the missions. Despite its narrative gestures toward subverting the gang as a possible social adaptation, the game situates the story missions as small accidents in the broader urban logic. As the player exits the open urban environment and reenters the missions, he or she does so willingly, and not under the duress of a complex historico-social precondition. This rhetoric implicitly affirms the metaphor of criminal behavior as moral depravity.

Whether *San Andreas's* creators intended the game to support or critique contemporary conservative American ideological structures is an open question. But the fact that the game has been so universally reviled, not only by the "values-oriented" conservative right but also by pillars of contemporary centrist politics, such as senators Hillary Clinton and Joseph Lieberman, suggests that neither side has actually played the game. How surprised would the conservatives be to find that a group of Scottish game developers may have placed tens of millions of copies of conservative political rhetoric in the waiting hands of contemporary American youth. This includes many inner-city youth who would normally be predisposed to oppose Republicans' pro-business, antisocial program stances. And how surprised might liberals be to find that they might have the perfect object lesson for counteracting conservative frames about poverty, class, race, and crime already installed on the nation's PlayStations. Even so, unexpected ideological frames similar to those implicated in *Grand Theft Auto: San Andreas* do not necessarily indicate that commercial developers have a hidden political agenda. For better or worse, it is much more likely that they are unaware that the procedural interaction in the game can imply a particular ideological stance. Market forces are unlikely to expose such failing as imprudence, and thus the task of unpacking ideology in games like *San Andreas* will become the work of the critic.

DESIGN FUTURES FOR POLITICAL GAMES

Politicians are already familiar with Lakoff's (1996) and Luntz's (2004) strategies on framing political speech, especially public speech. Those who wish to create videogames as endorsed or disruptive political speech will undoubtedly need to pay more attention to the use of context in such games. A shift away from verbal and toward procedural contextualization in such games will likely take longer. Lakoff (1996) argued that the central role in contemporary politics (and he has progressive politics in mind in particular) is to breathe new life into an otherwise bankrupt political discourse. This restructuring is necessary because citizens assume language and its carriers—from politicians to news media—are neutral. The public has little purchase on the "moral conceptual systems" that underwrite verbal and written political utterances themselves. Understanding a political position, argued Lakoff, "requires fitting it into an unconscious matrix of family-based morality" (p. 384). It is worth noting the urgent and somewhat desperate note on which Lakoff ended *Moral Politics: How Liberals and Conservatives Think*:

> In short, public discourse as it currently exists is not very congenial to the discussion of the findings of this study. Analysis of metaphor and the idea of alternative conceptual systems are not part of public discourse. Most people do not even know that they have conceptual systems, much less how they are structured. This does not mean that the characterizations of conservatism and liberalism in this book cannot be discussed publicly. They can and should be. What requires special effort is discussing the unconscious conceptual framework behind the discussion. (pp. 387–388)

Lakoff (2004) called this process frame shifting. Perhaps the most promising future political role of videogames will serve to help citizens take on precisely this challenge. As procedural systems, videogames are the only medium of mass appeal across many ages, demographics, and social–ethnic backgrounds that rely on conceptual frameworks—rule-based interactions—as their core mode of signification. We do not find it surprising when films like *Farenheit 9/11* (Moore, 2004) or television series such as *The Daily Show* (Smithberg & Winstead, 1996) make explicit, outright attempts to change political affinity. This is not yet the case for videogames. But unlike consumers of film, television, books, and other linear media, videogame players are accustomed to analyzing the interaction of proceduralized logic as a part of the play experience. John C. Beck and Mitchell Wade (2004) called this process "going meta" (p. 167), and they argued that it is changing the way a whole generation raised on games approaches business problems. Although particular political interests have effectively colonized some media—liberals and documentary film, conservatives and talk radio, for example—videogames remain indefinite about their political bent. This situation underscores a promise and a threat. On the one hand, the medium of the videogame has not (yet) become attached to a particular worldview; thus welcoming all varieties of ideological frames. On the other hand, lessons from other media have suggested that the political groups with stronger media strategies effectively lock out other voices. The questionable success of liberal talk radio station Air America provides an instructive example. The left has been effectively banished from the airwaves because the conservatives became entrenched on them so much earlier. Although it is first an analysis of political discourse, George Lakoff's (1996) *Moral Politics: How Liberals and Conservatives Think* could equally be described as a scathing critique on the failure of liberal political discourse. Perhaps today it seems Pollyannaish to claim that videogames might offer the most salient locus for discussions of how we think about political problems. But in time, and not much of it in my view, we will wonder why it took so long to realize that games had been a part of public political discourse, all along. And when that time comes, it would be unfortunate for one set of political positions to have so colonized the medium as to taint it for dissenting opinion.

REFERENCES

Austin, J. L. (1962). *How to do things with words*. Cambridge, MA: Harvard University Press.

Barbu, L. (1991). Crisis in the Kremlin. [Computer software]. Alameda, CA: Spectrum Holobyte.

Beck, J. C., & Wade, M. (2004). *Got game: How the gamer generation is reshaping business forever.* Cambridge, MA: Harvard Business School Press.

Bogost, I. (2004a). *Activism: The public policy game*. Atlanta, GA: Persuasive Games.

Bogost, I. (2004b). *Take back Illinois*. Atlanta, GA: Persuasive Games/Illinois House Republicans.

Bogost, I. (2006). *Unit operations: An approach to videogame criticism*. Cambridge, MA: MIT Press.

Bogost, I., & Frasca, G. (2003). *The Howard Dean for Iowa game*. Burlington, VT: Dean for America.

Booth, W. (2001, January 8). For Norton, a party mission. *The Washington Post*, p. A01.

Cart, J. (2003, January 21). Bush opens way for counties and states to claim wilderness roads. *The Los Angeles Times*, p. 1.

Carter, C. (Director). (1993). *The X-Files* [Television series]. Los Angeles, CA: Fox.

Crawford, C. (1985). Balance of power. [Computer software]. Novato, CA: Mindscape.

Crawford, C. (1990). *Balance of the planet*. Author.

Emmerich, R. (Director). (1996). *Independence day* [Motion picture]. Los Angeles, CA: Fox.

Frasca, G. (2003). *September 12*. Montevideo, Uruguay: Newsgaming.com.

Frasca, G. (2004). *Cambiemos*. Montevideo, Uruguay: Frente Amplio Nueva Mayoria/Powerful Robot Games.

Lakoff, G. (1990). *Women, fire, and dangerous things*. Chicago: University of Chicago Press.

Lakoff, G. (1996). *Moral politics: How liberals and conservatives think*. Chicago: University of Chicago Press.

Lakoff, G. (2004). *Don't think of an elephant: Know your values and frame the debate—The essential guide for progressives*. New York: Chelsea Green.

Lakoff, G., & Johnson, M. (1980). *Metaphors we live by*. Chicago: University of Chicago Press.

Le Chevallier, M. (2000). *Vigilance 1.0*. Helsinki: Kiasma Museum.

Luntz, F. I. (2002). *Energy, preparing for the future*. Alexandria, VA: Luntz Research Companies.

Luntz, F. I. (2003). *The environment: A cleaner, safer, healthier America*. Alexandria, VA: Luntz Research Companies.

Luntz, F. I. (2004). *The best and worst language of 2004: Key debate phrases*. Alexandria, VA: Luntz Research Companies.

Marinucci, C. (2004, November 7). In postmortem on Kerry bid, Dems seek clues to new life. *The San Francisco Chronicle*, p. A1.

Markel, H. (2003). Fast food, obesity, and hospitals. *Medscape Pediatrics, 5*(2).

Mateas, M., & Stern, A. (2002). A behavior language for story-based believable agents. *IEEE Intelligent Systems, 7*(4), 39–47.

Maxis. (1990). Sim earth. [Computer software]. Alameda, CA: Microprose.

Moore, M. (Director). (2004). *Farenheit 9/11* [Motion picture]. Culver City, CA: Sony Pictures.

National Environmental Trust. (2003). *Luntzspeak.com.* Retrieved October 10, 2005, from http://www.luntzspeak.com

Nestle, M. (2002). *Food politics: How the food industry influences nutrition and health.* Berkeley, CA: University of California Press.

Nestle, M. (2003). Increasing portion sizes in American diets: More calories, more obesity. *Journal of the American Dietetic Association, 103,* 231–234.

On, J. (2001). Antiwargame. [Computer software]. San Francisco: Futurefarmers.

Republican National Committee. (2004). *Tax invaders.* Washington, DC: Author.

Reuters. (2005). *Minister: Bush must be "shot down."* Retrieved October 10, 2005, from http://www.cnn.com/2005/WORLD/europe/09/08/germany.bush.reut/

Rockstar Games. (2001). Grand theft auto III. [Computer software]. New York: Take Two Interactive.

Rockstar Games. (2003). Grand theft auto: Vice City. [Computer software]. New York: Take Two Interactive.

Rockstar Games. (2004). Grand theft auto: San Andreas. [Computer software]. New York: Take Two Interactive.

Schifferes, S. (2004a, November 3). *Election reveals divided nation.* London, UK: BBC News.

Schifferes, S. (2004b, November 3). *What next for the Democrats.* London, UK: BBC News.

Searle, J. (1969). *Speech acts: An essay in the philosophy of language.* Cambridge, England: Cambridge University Press.

Smithberg, M., & Winstead, L. (Creators). (1996). *The daily show* [Television series]. New York, NY: Comedy Central.

Spurlock, M. (Director). (2004). *Super size me* [Motion picture]: Hard Sharp.

Taito. (1978). *Space invaders.* [Videogame]. Tokyo: Author.

Vanderbei, R. J. (2004). *Election 2004 results.* Retrieved October 10, 2005, from http://www.princeton.edu/~rvdb/JAVA/election2004/

Wallsten, P., & Anderson, N. (2004, November 6). Democrats map out a different strategy. *Los Angeles Times.*

Wells, H. G. (1898). *The war of the worlds.* New York: Aerie.

POPULAR COMMUNICATION, *4*(3), 185–202

Toward a Cultural Theory of Gaming: Digital Games and the Co-Evolution of Media, Mind, and Culture

Janet H. Murray

Georgia Institute of Technology

Digital games are an expanding popular cultural form and the focus of a new field of scholarship that has been concerned with defining games and establishing boundaries between games and other phenomena. Studies of the coevolution of human cognition and culture can throw light on this discussion by putting gaming into a longer human perspective. Although 2 chief theorists of this field, Michael Tomasello and Merlin Donald, have not explicitly focused on games, their work has suggested that games could have played an important role in shaping the human mind and human culture, by expanding and preserving adaptive cultural patterns, furthering symbolic thinking, and expanding and preserving the expressiveness of symbolic media. Digital games can be understood as carrying on the same functions, using the new affordances of the computer.

As T.S. Eliot (1921) so famously remarked, "what happens when a new work of art is created is something that happens simultaneously to all the works of art which preceded it." Marshall McLuhan (1994) noted the same effect in the invention of a new medium: It changes how we see the media that preceded it. The invention and striking global popularity of the new genre of computer games within the new digital medium is having a similar effect, causing us to reconsider older cultural categories such as narrative, games, and play (Aarseth, 1997; Bolter & Grusin, 1999; Laurel, 1993; Manovich, 2001; Murray, 1997). The rapid growth and enormous popularity of computer-based games has made them an object of study in their own right and provoked an active critical discourse about the relation of digital games to earlier media traditions and especially to narrative and film (Wardrip-Fruin & Harrigan, 2004). Some theorists, often called "ludologists," have argued that digital games can

Correspondence should be addresssed to Janet H. Murray, Literature, Communication, and Culture, Georgia Institute of Technology, Skiles 335, 686 Cherry Street, Atlanta, GA 30332. E-mail: janet.murray@lcc.gatech.edu best be understood as abstract rule systems, divorced from other cultural and symbolic content. In this view, the abstract game *Tetris* (1985) is the model for digital games, and the sexual attractiveness of a Lara Croft game figure or the player's sense of enacting a narrative with compelling characters and a happy or sad ending are irrelevant to the game experience (Aarseth, 2001, 2004; Eskelinen, 2001, 2004; Juul, 2001). For those like myself who believe the symbolic content of games is not so easily dismissed, the extreme formalist position of the ludologists is a useful challenge to clarify the role of symbolic content in gaming, and the connections between games and other cultural forms.

The field of digital game studies has established its own journals and research organizations including *Game Studies: The International Journal of Computer Game Research* and the Digital Games Research Association (n.d.), the latter of which describes itself as the "association for academics and professionals who research digital games and associated phenomena." Some within the field have dismissed the established research into play and games as having little to offer to an understanding of videogames. This is an understandable boundary, given the novelty of the new digital medium and the profound difference it has made in expanding the possibilities of representational forms in general, and of games in particular. However, work such as Brian Sutton-Smith's (1997) studies of children's games and his insightful synthesis of play theory, Bekoff and Byers's (1998) animal studies, and Parlett's (1999) formalistic studies of board games remain relevant to the study of computer games. Theorists who also are game designers explicitly connect the design of electronic games with the theory and practice of predigital gaming (Crawford, 2005; Salen & Zimmerman, 2003). This continuity also is recognized by formalist researchers who have sought to establish game typologies and taxonomies (Aarseth, Smedstad, & Sunnanå, 2003). For example, the "rock–paper–scissors" pattern of risks and trade-offs is a useful reference for describing similar computer game patterns involving three items (Bjork, Lundregn, & Holopainen, 2003).

The continuities between computer games and predigital games is evident in the popularity of computer-based versions of classics such as Solitaire and Scrabble, and in the growth of the videogame industry out of arcade play. We can see a progression from the shooting gallery to the pinball machine to the first person shooter or dancing game. The new encyclopedic, interactive digital medium makes extensive use of conventions from older media, reproducing game boards, playing fields, arcade weapons, vehicles as digital objects, animating human opponents as digital characters, and automating the scoring and rules systems. It also reproduces enduring behavioral patterns associated with gaming such as playfulness, tests of skill and strategy, competition, special rules and equipment, chance, spectacle, and a focus on performance (Caillois, 1961; Huizinga, 1949). The shape of videogames is, therefore, tied to older cultural forms and the pleasures of videogames seem to be rooted in our age-old attraction to games in general.

Games have not been treated as an expressive genre, such as theater, poetry, or folk songs. But their symbolic, social, and developmental value has been recognized in psychological, anthropological, and sociological studies. One obstacle to such disciplinary study is the notorious difficulty of defining games (Wittgenstein, 1958). Recent attempts to provide a definition of games as the basis for serious study of digital games have produced struggles with a few key outlier cases that make it difficult to see the boundaries between games and non-games. For example, we use the term "game" for nonplay activities such as simulation games and the stock market, and for activities that have real world consequences such as gambling (Juul, 2003). Similarly, some games such as baseball or crossword puzzles have endpoints with win–lose or solved–unsolved conditions, but others such as role-playing games or *The Sims* do not (Salen & Zimmerman, 2003). So games might best be described phenomenologically as a spectrum of playful ordered behavior that can be more or less playful and more or less ordered. However, such a solution runs into the even more contested category of play (Sutton-Smith, 1997).

The boundary between videogames and other forms of digital media is also becoming confusing. Videogames exploit all of the four key affordances of digital media: They are procedural, participatory, encyclopedic, and spatial (Murray, 1997). They include elaborate rule systems, rely on active intervention by the interactor and convene large numbers of simultaneous players, include vast amounts of information and multiple media forms, and offer complex spaces to move through. One might argue that digital games are becoming the assimilator of all earlier forms of media culture. They allow players to take on the characters of print fantasy literature or popular films. They incorporate cinematic characterization, lighting, camera angles, and even allow players to make their own movies within the game environment (a new narrative format called machinima). They include music, graphic design, and dialog, and they make wide use of narrative genres such as adventure, romance, gangsters, and superheroes and are rapidly assimilating other new media formats such as bulletin boards, chat rooms, and in-game newspapers and radio stations.

The general cultural pervasiveness of games that have made them so hard to define in the predigital world, has been magnified by the chameleon-like and expanding presence of the new digital games. This dramatic increase in the representational power, formal variety, and social impact of games increases the importance of understanding what games are and why we are drawn to playing them.

GAMES AS JOINT ATTENTIONAL SCENES

Our renewed interest in the distinguishing qualities of the ancient representational forms of games and narrative coincides with a moment of scientific focus and theoretical speculation on the prehistoric origins of mind and culture. One of the central puzzles of evolutionary theory is the problem of the short time span in which primates developed into humanoids and humanoids developed into human beings. The exact time frame of human evolution is still uncertain, but we know that we share 98% to 99% of our genes with our closest primate cousins, the bonobos and chimps, and there seems to be a scant 6 million years since the family tree diverged. Human-like creatures have only been around for about 2 million years. The last giant step in our evolution, which was largely cognitive and took us from homo sapiens to homo sapiens sapiens, seems to have lasted somewhere between 200,000 and 400,000 years, and seems to have ended as late as 50,000 years ago. These time steps are quite small in the 4-billion-year history of life on earth, and cognitive scientists face the challenge of explaining how we could have gotten so smart, compared to our close primate cousins, in such a short period. There does not seem to have been enough iterations of birth and adaptation and death, for natural selection to have created the dramatic advantages that we hold over other related species.

Michael Tomasello (2000) explained this compressed time scheme as the result of a single change in human cognition: the ability to understand cospecifics (other members of our species) as intentional agents like oneself. This foundational change underpins symbolic communication and allows us to engage in cultural learning. Culture is the key element here, because the human advantage over other species lies in our ability to share and transmit knowledge and patterns of behavior across historical time and in the raising of children.

To make clear the distinction between the cognition of humans and other primates who share much of our sensory experience and our social orientation, Tomasello (2000) listed five actions that nonhuman primates do not do in their natural habitats:

- Point or gesture to outside objects for others.
- Hold objects up to show them to others.
- Bring others to locations so they can observe things there.
- Actively offer objects to other individuals by holding them out.
- Intentionally teach other individuals new behaviors.

Human ontogeny, the development of the individual in childhood, seems to reproduce Tomasello's hypothesized phylogenic achievement. At about 9 months of age a baby begins to recognize when he or she has the parent's attention, and then is able to follow the parent's attention to external objects by following their gaze. By 15 months the baby usually has begun pointing at things to direct the parent's attention to objects of interest. Human infants below the age of 9 months, similar to nonhuman primates, have a limited concept of their conspecifics (members of their species) as having mental awareness and intentionality. But somewhere around their 1st birthday, human infants begin to understand other people as intentional agents or "animate beings who have goals and who make active choices among behavioral means for attaining these goals, including active choices about what to pay attention to in pursuing those goals" (Tomasello, 2000, p. 68). Tomasello further believes that the ability to follow on the attention of the adult leads to the child recognizing when he or she is his- or herself the focus of the adult's attention and gaze, and this begins to lay the framework for an understanding of the self as an actor in the social world. This cognitive leap, which happened for the species in relatively recent evolutionary time (the last 250,000 years or so) and for the individual at 9 to 15 months old, forms the basis for the communicative cultural tasks that make up the bulk of human achievement. It is the basis of sharing, negotiating, learning, and symbolic communication.

The framework in which the cognitive achievement of understanding intentionality leads to the acquisition of culturally transmitted knowledge is called a *joint attentional scene*. A joint attentional scene involves two participants, such as a parent and child, who both understand what the other is attending to. In babyhood it occurs in play or in caretaking situations when the adult and the child have a common interest (e.g., food, tickling, stroking, diapering) and exchange gestures, sounds, or looks that each recognizes as intentional and connected to whatever holds their common focus. Once a baby and its parent achieve this ability, the baby's learning increases exponentially. Tomasello (2000) similarly believes that once early humanoids achieved this ability the possibility for cultural breakthroughs increased exponentially.

Tomasello's (2000) insight into the development of human cognition may shed light on one of the more puzzling aspects of games: Why are they fun? What is the primary motivation to engage in them? We know that play is intrinsically pleasurable for animals and humans alike, and there are many theories about its evolutionary value, including rehearsal of adult skills and mastery of a flexible repertoire of responses (Bekoff & Byers, 1998; Sutton-Smith, 1997). We seem hardwired to play—to explore for the simple pleasure of exercising our faculties and exploring the world in nonsurvival ways. This exploratory play seems to serve the purpose of expanding our repertoire of responses and of offering a wider range of cognitive patterns to apply to new situations. But games explicitly limit and channel the intrinsically pleasurable exploration characteristic of play.

In fact, games often ask us to do things that would be work if we were required to do it. I am capable of spending 1 hour or more sorting and matching symbols in a game such as *Gem Drop,* and yet I would find it torture to have to do such tasks for a living. I have known graduate students who spent hours negotiating treaties for imaginary kingdoms in live action role-playing games or coordinating the activities of a team of adventurers in an online multiplayer game. As the administrator of an academic program, it is hard for me to see such tasks as recreation, but to the players they have all the features of a game. What is it about a game activity that is intrinsically enjoyable to those who choose to engage in it? What do games offer in return for limiting the exploratory delights of play?

Perhaps the enjoyment of games is hard-wired into us, selected by thousands of years of cultural behavior to encourage us to seek out situations similar to Tomasello's (2000) joint attentional scenes.

Indeed, the three defining characteristics of a joint attentional scene are similar to the social situation necessary for gaming:

- Shared limited focus on external objects or behaviors (or both)
- Mutually witnessed intentionality among participants within the shared context
- Symbolic communication between participants

The ability to form this joint attentional scene makes it possible to engage in the activities characteristic of games: to treat abstract representations consistently, behave according to negotiated rules, and limit one's actions and attention to the game pieces and game actions to what "counts" in the game by screening out other stimuli and actions. Joint attention organizes two of the core activities of games: turn taking and synchronizing behaviors.

Tomasello's (2000) theory also suggested some of the core adaptive benefits of games, because they reinforce key benefits of joint attentional scenes:

- An understanding of the self both as an agent and an object within a community of other intentional agent–objects
- The ability to shift perspective from one's own point of view to the point of view of others, to imagine what someone else is thinking, and to see oneself from the point of view of the other
- The ability to intentionally teach and learn, which is the foundation of all human cultural development

It is easy to think of a contemporary board game or one of its early precursors, such as mancala or knucklebones, as a joint attentional activity, composed of limited focus, mutually witnessed intentional acts, and symbolic manipulation. Taking turns dropping seeds into a special set of holes in the ground or throwing pieces of animal bone or clay dice, the players are aware of each one's turn, of each one's separate actions and history in the game, and of the relative position of each to one another in the scoring of the game. Watching one another play is an opportunity for passive and active learning, and for metacomments on the play of one another. Board games intensify the opportunity for witnessing the actions of the other player and for keeping track of multiple positions within the same game. Sports games intensify the opportunity for intentional teaching and learning by focusing performance on goal-centered behaviors that are optimized for comparison between players and between turns. Games provide a framework for watching and critiquing iterative activities and for working collectively for improved performance. These patterns of behavior are then available for survival activities.

If Tomasello (2000) was right, and our ability to form joint intentional scenes was a prerequisite to the acquisition of language, then games may be understood as a foundational element in human culture, as the gestural starting point in the history of representational media. Although he did not mention games, I believe Tomasello's work, considered in juxtaposition to other research on games and children's play, clearly points in this direction. For example, researchers at Duke University have studied toddler imitation games, such as taking turns jumping off a box, which are good examples of how joint attention is established and elaborated between cognitively matched, pre-linguistic children (Didow & Eckerman, 2001). For Carol Eckerman (Malcom, 2000) the important cognitive feature of these games is that they serve as a form of preverbal communication. She interpreted their mirroring interaction as a kind of dialog without language. I expect that the children are using imitation of nonverbal actions as a way of reaching agreement on a topic for their interaction. So, when one child imitates another he or she may say something similar to "let's do this together" and when the first child imitates back it is kind of similar to a confirmation: "Yes, I like this too."

Interestingly enough, Sutton-Smith (1997), citing Kenneth Burke and Gregory Bateson, made a similar suggestion about the function of play biting in animals. He suggested that play might be the earliest form of a negative, prior to the existence of the negative in language. Play, as a way of not doing whatever it represents, prevents error. It is a positive behavioral negative. It says no by saying yes. It is a bite but it is a nip (Sutton-Smith, 1997). In both cases, the urge to play is a means of communicating in a situation in which intelligent creatures have not yet acquired language. A play action is a signal similar to a predator call, except that its referent is to the social world.

Most interestingly, Eckerman (Malcom, 2000) observed how imitation games can lead to the development of language in clearly differentiated steps. To paraphrase and summarize her observations: First, they direct each other: "go," "wait," "jump," and "watch me." Then they answer one another: "my turn" and "you jump." Finally they describe their actions as they do them: "I jump" or "big jump!" while jumping off the box.

The game is organizing their behavior, and providing practice in language exchange and in synchronized expectations and performance. The pleasure of the game lies as much in the communication as in the actions, and it lies particularly in the matching of language to action, and in the choreographing of both into a patterned social interaction. The pleasure of games reinforces the adaptive behavior of symbolic communication around patterned social behaviors. Eckerman was particularly struck by the joyousness of the imitation game. Her work provides a dramatic parallel to Tomasello's (2000) hypothesized moments of evolutionary progress.

You can infer from the laughing and smiling going on that they really enjoy interacting with each other. Perhaps in these imitative interactions they are experiencing both their similarity to others and their separateness. Perhaps they are learning that we each are intentional agents of action and that playing together is a very pleasant thing (Malcom, 2000).

These early games are based on mutually elaborated patterns that serve the same purpose as written rules. They are intrinsically social and can, in fact, be understood as a celebration of the social—of the very presence of other intentional beings. The pleasure derived from sharing attention and witnessing and enacting intentional acts forms the framework for mastering complex physical and social skills. Spectatorship is as much a part of the experience as active performance, and in early games it is an alternating spectatorship: You do, I do; you do, I do. The elaboration of joint attentional scenes into ever more elaborate games sets up opportunities for performance, for presenting the self as a performer in a socially constructed arena, and for incorporating multiple individuals into flexible but predictable group structures.

Seeing the joint attentional scene as the ancestor of all games is another way of answering Wittgenstein's (1958) view of games as exemplary of how messy linguistic categories are. Wittgenstein complained that there is clearly nothing in common between board games, card games, or Olympic games, or between chess, tic-tac-toe, and tennis. Then he added his capper example: The least similar of all these examples is ring-a-ring-a-roses (as it is translated, or Ring Round Rosy, as it is more commonly called in the United States). Recent digital game theorists have argued that Wittgenstein gave up too soon, and they have offered their own definitions of games (Juul, 2003; Salen & Zimmerman, 2003). But they also have trouble making an inclusive definition (as discussed previously), and they exclude Ring Round Rosy because it does not have a winning condition. Yet in the light of Tomasello's (2000) and Eckerman's research, we can think of Ring Round Rosy as the paradigmatic game.

Ring Round Rosy is a variant on the toddler imitation games, but one that is taught rather than improvised, and it is one that is often led by adults, but which children then play on their own. The rhyme belongs to a relatively recent period, first appearing in print in the 19th century, and therefore not referring to the bubonic plague as some have suggested (Opie & Opie, 1973). But the activity of circling, making rhythmical noises, and obeying a symbolic verbal command to fall, could all be part of a preliterate early human game. Ring Round Rosy reflects many elements that make games valuable to the species and the individual that account for the adaptive value of the time that children put into playing them. It involves establishing a shared focus—a circle formed by everyone holding hands in which everyone is therefore focused on one another behaving in a mirroring way. It synchronizes the behavior of the group, which is one of the key requirements for survival in a culture of hunting. It creates a cohesive group, it enacts group cohesion, and reinforces identification with one another and recognition of one another as sharing perceptions and intentionality. The climax "all fall down" is the most difficult part of the game of course, and the pleasure is similar to the pleasure Eckerman's toddlers have in jumping off the box one after another, but with the added excitement achieving simultaneity.

THE COEVOLUTION OF GAMES, NARRATIVE, AND MEDIA

Thinking of games in terms of their possible evolutionary history (their adaptive value) helps us to think about the persistent conflict in game studies between those who emphasize the similarities between games and stories and those who emphasize their differences (Wardrip-Fruin & Harrigan, 2004). It is significant that Tomasello (2000) linked the uniquely human understanding of cospecifics' consciousness with the uniquely human understanding of other unseen underlying causes. Tomasello believed that "human causal understanding evolved first in the social domain to comprehend others as social agents." Although there is "no way of knowing if this is true," he pointed to the cultural evidence that "many of the people of the world, when they are in doubt as to the physical cause of an event, often invoke various types of animistic or deistic forces to explain it; perhaps this is the default approach" (p. 24). In other words, sensing the unseen intentions of other people is linked to an animistic view of the world that creates explanatory narratives of intention for other events as well. Cognitive theorist Mark Turner (1996) would have agreed that an abstract sense of cause and effect is an early human cognitive achievement and precedes the acquisition of language. Turner explicitly identified this cognitive leap as narrative or "parable" making: the abstraction of causal sequences from the observed world. If we accept these theories of early cognition then we can think of games and stories as driving and coevolving with the development of language, leading to the development of more complex social patterns, more complex causal thinking, and more elaborate symbolic culture.

The Tomasello (2000) hypothesis can be interpreted as linking both games and stories to the single moment in which human consciousness first awakened. The moment has two key aspects:

- The understanding of one's fellow creatures as intentional beings, leading to the exploration of joint attention, *which can be understood as the birth of mimetic games*
- The understanding of overt events as the result of invisible causes, which leads to abstract thinking about causal patterns, *which can be understood as the birth of narrative thinking*

These two cognitive and cultural advances have one key effect: the elaboration of symbolic communication, starting with gesture and vocalization and developing into spoken language, *which can be understood as the birth of media.*

The previous italicized phrases represent my interpretation of Tomasello's (2000) theory. Just as culture and cognition coevolve, I argue that the elements of culture are also subject to an ongoing process of coevolution. Mimetic games lead to greater social organization and closer attention to the world, which forwards causal thinking, which leads to more complicated games—both of which produce a demand for more expressive language. This pattern—the coevolution of games, narrative, and language—is visible in toddlers and children. It is imaginable as a narrative of prehistoric human life. It also is visible in the cultural patterns of historical time if we think of human (spoken) language as a medium, and of later symbolic media as coevolving in a similar way with ever more elaborate mimetic and causal (game and story) genres. To knit these different time scales together and motivate these rather broad generalizations, it is useful to turn to the work of Merlin Donald (1991).

Games are hardly mentioned in Donald's (1991) theories of the coevolution of cognition and culture, but his framework, similar to Tomasello's (2000), provides a useful way of thinking about the role they have played. Donald hypothesized that modern human cognition arose in four steps. It started with *episodic culture* (the split from our primate cousins), which we share with other mammals and primates, in which social relationships and even simple tool use develop on the basis of brain function that allows only discrete episodic structure and recall. *Mimetic culture* is the step in which the early hominids can understand one another as intentional, conscious agents and can communicate symbolically. This allows them to form bands, migrate, hunt, make domesticate fire, and make simple tools. *Mythic culture* is when sapient humans communicate through symbolic forms of representation such as oral language, mimetic rituals, and cave paintings. They understand the world in narrative terms. Modern *theoretical culture* is understanding the world in terms of abstract formalisms and is based on massive externally stored memory systems such as print and computers.

The transition between the first and second stage is the one Tomasello (2000) described as bringing an understanding of shared attention and abstract causes. The mimetic stage can be thought of as driven by games and rituals, the elaboration of the synchronized actions, and communications of the humanoids with a capacity for joint attention. Game playing in this stage may have been mostly tied to survival, with the pleasure of synchronization adding energy to the acquisition of skills necessary for evading predatory animals or collectively hunting them. A sustained culture of rule-based coordinated behaviors would reinforce the development of language, which in turn would support more detailed and memorable stories. Mimetic behaviors survive in contemporary society, in pleasurable rituals such as dancing and athletics. The earliest videogames were mimetic in that the game play was focused on the mastery of simple repetitive behaviors, moving a character through a maze and "eating" pellets. With the elaboration of the medium of videogames to include more detailed graphics and more responsive and complex programming, videogames offer us more complex patterns to absorb and perform. The toddler's pleasure in joint attention and imitation is reproduced in a way by games that challenge us to synchronize our actions with machines, such as the arcade game *Dance Dance Revolution* (Konami, 1998), in which players must keep up with a pattern of dance steps. Similar to an oral culture game such as *Simon Says,* which challenges children to conform their behavior to symbolic codes (spoken commands), *Dance Dance Revolution* presents the dance steps not by example, but in a spatial notation that must be quickly interpreted and acted on. Games such as these may help us to elaborate a common symbolic language with our new electronic joint attentional partners.

The third stage, mythic culture, can be seen as driven by complex narratives—the result of more elaborated oral language and longer traditions of shared experience. Mythic thinking, characterized by heroic legends and ritually transmitted narratives, is apparent in the writings of antiquity that transcribe oral sources and in preliterate cultures. But forms of mythic thinking endure into our postliterate age, often reinforcing affiliations based on common identities as in families, ethnic groups, and political parties. When athletic events become mass spectator sports in which players embody the aspirations of spectator fans, they pass from mimetic into mythic culture, with larger than life performances of super human beings. Videogames often invoke this mythic state of mind by casting the player in the role of superhero or placing the action within a fantasy domain characterized by animism and supernatural "mythical" figures.

The fourth and current stage of human culture, according to Donald (1991), is characterized by theoretical thinking. The transition from the mythic to the theoretical stage is the result of the invention of writing, which was first used as a commercial tool and for talismanic inscriptions of the names of gods and rules. Later it was a way of recording oral culture such as stories and magical spells. It was then perfected by the Greeks as a means of recording the process of thinking and reasoning, thereby allowing for a sustained collective discourse that moves from mythic explanations to reasoned argumentation. In Donald's elegant analysis we move from ape to Einstein in only three steps, which we can think of in terms of symbolic exchange, cognitive strategies, or cultural building blocks: from joint attention to language to writing, from mimesis to narrative to argumentation, and from ritual to myth to theory.

Although neither Tomasello (2000) or Donald (1991) pointed to games as instruments of cognitive evolution, it is striking how often games are part of their arguments. Tomasello's experimental examples with apes and children have usually been in the form of games. Both Tomasello and Donald pointed to children's superiority at games as evidence of fundamental cognitive differences that predate language acquisition.

Human children play rule-governed games by imitation, often without any formalized instruction. They invent and learn new games, often without using language. Apes, similar to other animals, cannot learn similar games. Apes are restricted to games that, by our standards, are very simple. The problem of bridging from ape to human would thus appear to involve a great deal more than pinpointing the arrival time of vocal language (Donald, 1991). But although Donald instanced mimetic games as one of the key components of hominid development, both cognitive scientists stopped short of seeing games as a driving force of cognitive and cultural evolution. Yet the more one thinks about the elements of cultural cognition the more game-like they seem.

GAMES AS CULTURAL RATCHETS

Tomasello (2000) and others accounted for the rapid progress of human culture over a relatively brief time span as benefiting from "the ratchet effect." The process of cumulative cultural evolution requires not only creative invention but also, and just as importantly, faithful social transmission that can work as a ratchet to prevent slippage backward. This is so that the newly invented artifact or practice preserves its new and improved form at least somewhat faithfully until a further modification or improvement comes along (Tomasello, 2000, p. 5).

Games seem to be well-suited to the role of cultural ratchet, preserving patterns of behavior from one generation to the next through the intrinsic pleasure of shared attention and imitation. Game play in itself is a means of transmitting general habits of imitating, sequencing, and synchronizing actions. In a mimetic culture, games may have provided practice in linking language to objects and actions. In a mythic culture, they linked the practice of augury with numerical skills through symbolic gambling games. An ancient game such as mancala, which can be played with seeds and holes in the earth, can serve as a framework for practicing and preserving cognitive skills such as sorting and social skills such as turn taking and bluffing. Many patterns that are rigidly enforced in games are also the basis of general social organization, such as turn taking, following the leader, exchanging property, team formation, conflict containment, and collective focusing on common goals. The win–lose pattern of games seems also to be adaptive in motivating repeated practice and competitive effort.

The formal structure of games as participatory rule systems also can be seen as functioning as a cultural ratchet. The rules of games allow social groups to focus questions of what is allowed, disallowed, fair, and unfair. They offer a symmetrical means of interaction—a way of practicing reciprocity. Games involve a pleasure in inventing, establishing, recognizing, and reproducing patterns of behavior and object manipulation. This close attention to pattern and delight in pattern mimicry has survival value as the basis of skill acquisition and social organization. It is still the case that we experience nonplay situations as games, meaning that they are enjoyable or compelling as abstract patterns of interaction, when they have clear rule systems, especially those involving relative gain and loss, such as the stock market; the legal system; or even, disturbingly, warfare.

Other game patterns seem to address basic cognitive skills such as sequencing actions, coordinating hand and eye, sorting, matching, counting, and navigating a map. These game primitives are common to the earliest children's games and to traditional games including those known from ancient times, such as athletic contests, dice, and board games. They all focus attention on a limited domain and force us to match our behavior with conscious, shared expectations.

As Donald (1991) pointed out, human cognitive advancement is closely linked to the development of media of communication. Mimetic gestural exchange within the context of joint attentional scenes is a kind of prelinguistic medium. Language brings an exponential increase in our capacity for symbolic representation. Writing increases our ability to order the world, retain consistency of practices over time, record and retrieve information, and shape sustained arguments. But modern theoretical culture requires the massive storage of information and sustained arguments over longer periods of time.

Games have been, and continue to be, useful in directing our attention to all of these media, allowing for exploration of new means of expression and preserving outdated media forms for later reuse. Games can be seen as a means of coevolving our minds and our media, of assimilating new technologies of inscription through exploration of their capacity for symbolic representation, and of preserving and expanding symbolic expression by making symbolic systems the explicit focus of activity.

Board games from tic tac toe to chess allow us to focus on the common interpretation of inscriptions, which is the basis of written language. Games offer practice in symbolic media and often focus on the symbol making. For example riddle games, puns, and nonsense rhymes foreground the arbitrary linkages between sound and meaning in the medium of spoken language. Game tokens hearken back to an archaic counting system, invented ten thousand years ago that was the forerunner of cuneiform writing. Clay tokens shaped like spheres, cones, cylinders, rectangles, and other distinct forms represented commodities such as jugs of wine or heads of sheep in the nascent economies of Near East. Around 3500 B.C. clay envelope-like containers began to appear, marked with token-shaped imprints. By about 3200 B.C. these containers had evolved into clay tablets imprinted with cuneiform symbols (Schmandt-Besserat, 1996). This progression from token to tablet is echoed in the earliest preserved board game, the Royal Game of Ur (c. 2600 B.C.), which includes round tokens with geometrically grouped marking and a playing board divided into squares with similar markings. Progress around the board (it seems to have been a race game) was controlled by throwing three pyramid shaped dice, which are believed to have had binary values (0 or 1). Similar to the token system, dice (or lots) are among the oldest symbolic media in the world, associated in ancient times with divination, fate, and gambling. The backgammon board resembles accounting tables that functioned as aids to calculation. The use of the computer as an automated game board repeats these patterns both literally and formally: It incorporates images of ancient game boards, and it follows the same pattern of domesticating complex media through game-like exploration.

Digital Games as Cultural and Media Vanguards

I have argued elsewhere that the advent of the computer as a medium with its unique combination of procedural, participatory, encyclopedic, and spatial affordances is an advance in human culture comparable to the invention of print or moving image photography (Murray, 1997). The new digital medium expands our cognitive powers by offering us new ways of representing the world (e.g., through parameterized simulations) and greater powers of organizing information (e.g., multimedia archives accessible through metadata). It also is a medium that is particularly well-suited to games, because the rules of the game can be programmed into the computer and because the user can take on the role of the player. Playing games on the computer is similar to, and different from, predigital game playing. It conflates game and puzzle into a single form in that a game played against a mechanized opponent is really a procedural puzzle. It can eliminate turn taking by providing worlds that are always open to interruption and intervention at whatever pace the interactor is willing or able to sustain. The computer is not aware of our common focus because it is not conscious in the same way a human player is conscious. But it provides us with a partner whose thought processes we are aware of, and who represents the mediated consciousness of an implied human programmer. We engage with the computer as if it were an embodied opponent, but also as if it were similar to a painting or a book—the result of a prior act of conscious representation. Games can be thought of as socializing us into a new cyborg order, establishing rituals of commonality with proceduralized artifacts.

Digital games also capture the promise of digital media to exponentially expand the information- rich representational structures on which our modern culture rests. They let us play with complex representations that are similar to the system models we are building in every domain of human knowledge, from cosmology to global finance to family psychology. The design of *Sim City* (Wright, 1989), for example, rests on models similar to those used by urban planners. Although critics have contested the social assumptions behind those models, the game play provides us with a way of thinking about the interrelatedness of resources within a city and the multiple possible ways a city can grow (Friedman, 1999; Starr, 1994). The cognitive strategies and representational conventions of the systems mode of thought are spread by simulation games such as *Sim City,* just as games in older media forms spread older visual, verbal, and numerical skills sets and conventions. As the medium in which we create such models becomes more plastic and accessible, we may develop ways of exchanging alternate interactive models of the same phenomena, just as we have developed ways of spreading alternate sequences of verbal reasoning through oral and print culture.

Games also are the means of elaborating and practicing rituals of social organization. The Internet has extended the social power of gaming by allowing hundreds of thousands of people to participate in shared rule-based communities, starting with the text-based "multiplayer dungeons" of the 1980s. The Korean game *Lineage* (Song, 2001) attracts millions of players and lasts over years; *Everquest* (Verant, 1999) and *World of Warcraft* (Blizzard, 2004) sustain hundreds of thousands of players. A common element of these worlds is the negotiation of social rules of behavior, such as property rights and player-against-player killing. Online communities also self- organize around puzzle games such as the one released in connection with Steven Spielberg's (2001) film *AI*. The new category of pervasive games combines Web and mobile communication technologies with geographical positioning to take established game forms such as scavenger hunts and participatory theater into our new information spaces, and to blur the boundaries between the real and the virtual. This massive, team-oriented global gaming activity is an accompaniment to the many global-scale cultural, social, and political processes that characterize the early 21st century.

Games have also become a focus of participatory performance art, calling attention to symbolic content of games often in disturbing ways. The British art collective Blast Theory produces unsettling treasure hunts in virtual and real urban space that require the player to trust strangers (http://www.blasttheory.co.uk). Avant Gaming has announced a reinvention of the arcade game *Dance Dance Revolution* (2001) into *Dance Dance Immolation,* in which players wearing aluminized protective fire suits are rewarded for skillful dancing by propane guns shooting flames in the air and punished by having the flames aimed at the player's face. Although mainstream game design has its fixed genres and predictable titles, the audience is sophisticated enough to recognize the work of auteurs such as Will Wright and Peter Molyneux and to savor innovation in the aesthetics of game play. One of the most popular digital games of the past few years is *Katamari Damacy* (Takahashi, 2004), a hypnotic and surreal screen-based game, in which the player rolls a ball that picks up everything it comes in contact with—furniture, trees, buildings—until it reaches global proportions. Although the designer, Keita Takahashi, was inspired by Japanese children's ball rolling games, the world of the game is quite original, bizarrely supernatural without being conventionally heroic or gothic. The fantasy quality of this world derives from the powerful movement of the ball, which is simply and logically displayed in the virtual world, and yet unimaginable in the world of real objects. *Katamari Damacy*, similar to the wildly popular abstract game, *Tetris* (Pajitnov, 1985), challenges us to develop new spatial manipulation skills by creating compelling concrete images that behave in unreal but logical ways.

The work of Tomasello (2000) and Donald (1991) invites us to think about the history of human cognition as based on a succession of symbolic media patterns: Mimesis brings us language that brings us mythic narrative that brings us writing that brings us theoretical discourse that now brings us the computer. Yet all of these media stages are present at any time because they represent persistent, productive cultural strategies. In fact, we can think of the superset of all media as a single language, a paradigm of symbolic communication, and a union catalog of expressive symbols of every kind. As a species we are in possession of this symbol set, and we are constantly inventing new patterns to express new experiences or previously unseen or unspoken or untheorized phenomena. Our media are coevolving with our collective mind and culture. Donald adopted Vygotsky's (1978) notion of the zone of proximal development to speak about a zone of *proximal evolution,* the space between primate and human cognition or between different stages of human cognition. I would add the concept of a zone of proximal media evolution: a next stage of potential invention for the technologies and conventions of symbolic communication. In the 19th century, the movies were in this zone—capable of being invented because of the convergence of new technologies with ancient story patterns. Similarly, the turn of the 21st century has seen the invention of the multimedia networked computer and the emergence of videogames drawing on millennia of game conventions. In the collective process of inventing new symbolic media forms, we rely on the scaffolding of older media and patterns drawn from other activities. Games are a form of pattern abstraction that has served us well over thousands of years. They are the means of divorcing behaviors and symbols from their real world context and manipulating them as pure symbol systems: Tokens no longer represent sheep, but just a system of exchange across a game board. The computer is the most capacious pattern-making medium we have ever had. We have only begun to glimpse the new symbolic structures that we can build with it: cognitive scaffolds that will help us to organize and advance the traditions of thinking that have now brought us beyond the ability to represent our ideas in purely linear form. Given that games play a key role in giving birth to language in the individual and the species, we should not be surprised that they are playing a key role in elaborating the new symbolic language of interaction, in expanding the zone of proximal development for digital media.

The computer is the quintessential medium of theoretical discourse, but it also brings us back to the basics of mimetic representation. In some ways it is the machine whose attention we are sharing and whose primitive cognition we are cultivating with our expanding repertoire of ritual behaviors. It is tempting to see the current moment as parallel to the origin stories we have been elaborating. Just as games led us away from our primate cousins and into the richly meaningful human world of symbolic culture, so they seem now to be leading us into a new intimacy with the machine. Is the zone of proximal media evolution filled with cyborg creatures waiting to be born? The answer lies, perhaps, in the joyful source of cultural development—the toddler's pleasure in recognizing companionship and coordinating action. Although computers may crash with maddening regularity, they never do it for fun. Although they may act with magnificent global coordination, they do not do it for the joy of it. In other words, it is foolish to worry about people being supplanted by a chess-playing program (which is after all a triumph of the very human activity of symbolic representation). We should instead ask ourselves if it is likely that two laptops, idle and side by side, will one day generate a binary version of Ring Round Rosy.

REFERENCES

Aarseth, E. (1997). *Cybertext: Perspectives on ergodic literature.* Baltimore: Johns Hopkins University Press.

Aarseth, E. (2001, February). Computer game studies, year one. *Game Studies, 1*(1). Retrieved June 5, 2005, from http://www.gamestudies.org/0101/editorial.html

Aarseth, E. (2004). Genre trouble: Narrativism and the art of simulation. In N. Wardrip-Fruin & P. Harrington (Eds.), *First person: New media as story, performance, and game* (pp. 45–47). Cambridge, MA: MIT Press.

Aarseth, E., Smedstad, S. M., & Sunnanå, L. (2003). A multidimensional typology of games. In M. Copier & J. Raessens (Eds.), *Level up: Digital Games Research Association Conference Proceedings* (pp. 48–53). The Netherlands: Utrecht University. Retrieved January 25, 2006, from http://www.digra.org/dl/db/05163.52481

Bekoff, M., & Byers, J. A. (Eds.). (1998). *Animal play: Evolutionary, comparative, and ecological perspectives.* New York: Cambridge University Press.

Bjork, S., Lundregn, S., & Holopainen, J. (2003). Game design patterns. In *Level up: Digital Games Research Association Conference Proceedings* (pp. 180–193). The Netherlands: Utrecht University. Retrieved January 25, 2006, from http://www.digra.org/dl/db/05163.15303

Blizzard. (2005). World of warcraft. [Computer software]. Korea: Blizzard Entertainment.

Bolter, J., & Grusin, R. (1999). *Remediation: Understanding new media.* Cambridge, MA: MIT Press.

Breznican, A. (2004). Spielberg, Zemekis say video games, film could become one. *Associated Press, San Diego Union-Tribune.*

Caillois, R. (1961). *Man, play, and games.* (M. Barash, Trans.). New York: Free Press. (Original work published 1958)

Crawford, C. (2005). *Chris Crawford on interactive storytelling.* Berkeley, CA: New Riders.

Didow, S. M., & Eckerman, C. O. (2001). Toddler peers: From nonverbal coordinated action to verbal discourse. *Social Development, 10*(2), 170–188.

Donald, M. (1991). *Origins of the modern mind: Three stages in the evolution of culture and cognition.* Cambridge, MA: Harvard University Press.

Eliot, T. S. (1921). Tradition and the individual talent. In *The sacred wood: Essays on poetry and criticism* (chap. 8). New York: Knopf.

Eskelinen, M. (2001, July). The gaming situation. *Game Studies, 1*(1). Retrieved June 5, 2005, from http://www.gamestudies.org/0101/eskelinen/

Eskelinen, M. (2004). Toward computer game studies. In N. Wardrip-Fruin & P. Harrington (Eds.), *First person: New media as story, performance, and game* (pp. 36–49). Cambridge, MA: MIT Press.

Friedman, T. (1999, April 15). The semiotics of SimCity. *First Monday, 4*(4). Retrieved June 5, 2005, from http://www.firstmonday.org/issues/issue4_4/friedman/index.html

Game Studies. (n.d.). http://www.gamestudies.org.

Huizinga, J. (1980). *Homo ludens: A study of the play-element in culture.* (R. F. C. Hull, Trans.). London: Routledge & Kegan Paul. (Original work published 1938)

Juul, J. (2001, July). Games telling stories? A brief note on games and narratives. *Game Studies, 1*(1). Retrieved June 5, 2005, from http://www.gamestudies.org/0101/juul-gts/

Juul, J. (2003). The game, the player, the world: Looking for a heart of gameness. In M. Copier & J. Raessens (Eds.), *Level up: Digital Games Research Association Conference Proceedings* (pp. 30–45). The Netherlands: Utrecht University. Retrieved January 25, 2006, from http://www.digra.org/dl/db05163.50560

Konami. (1998). Dance dance revolution. [Computer software]. Author.

Laurel, B. (1993). *Computers as theatre.* Reading, MA: Addison-Wesley.

Malcom, K. (2000, June 30). Studies shed light on toddler development. *Duke News.* Retrieved June 5, 2005, from http://www.dukenews.duke.edu/2000/06/toddler630_print.htm

Manovich, L. (2001). *The language of new media.* Cambridge, MA: MIT Press.

McLuhan, M. (1994). *Understanding media: The extensions of man.* Cambridge, MA: MIT Press.

Murray, J. H. (1997). *Hamlet on the holodeck: The future of narrative in cyberspace.* New York: Free Press.

Opie, I. A., & Opie, P. (Eds.). (1973). *The Oxford dictionary of nursery rhymes.* Oxford, England: Clarendon.

Pajitnov, A. (1985). Tetris. [Computer software]. Various.

Parlett, D. S. (1999). *The Oxford history of board games.* New York: Oxford University Press.

Salen, K., & Zimmerman, E. (2003). *Rules of play: Game design fundamentals.* Cambridge, MA: MIT Press.

Schmandt-Besserat, D. (1996). *How writing came about.* Austin: University of Texas Press.

Song, J. (1998). Lineage. [Computer software]. Seoul, Korea: NCSoft.

Starr, P. (1994, March 21). Seductions of sim: Policy as a simulation game. *American Prospect, 5*(17), 19–29.

Sutton-Smith, B. (1997). *The ambiguity of play.* Cambridge, MA: Harvard University Press.

Takahashi, K. (2004). Katamari damacy. [Computer software]. Tokyo, Japan: Namco.

Tomasello, M. (2000). *The cultural origins of human cognition.* Cambridge, MA: Harvard University Press.

Turner, M. (1996). *The literary mind: The origins of thought and language.* New York, Oxford: Oxford UP.

Verant. (1999). Everquest. [Computer software]. Sony Online Entertainment.

Vygotsky, L. S. (1978). *Mind and society: The development of higher mental processes.* Cambridge, MA: Harvard University Press.

Wardrip-Fruin, N., & Harrigan, P. (Eds.). (2004). *First person: New media as story, performance, and game.* Cambridge, MA: MIT Press.

Wittgenstein, L. (1958). *Philosophical investigations* (3rd ed.). (G. E. M. Anscombe, Trans.). New York: MacMillan. (Original work published 1953)

Wright, W. (1989). Sim city. [Computer software]. Maxis Software.

POPULAR COMMUNICATION, 4(3), 203–211

The Culture and Business of Cross-Media Productions

Espen Aarseth

IT–University of Copenhagen

Risk-adverse producers and investors seek to capitalize on marketing by co-launching concepts through multiple media: the game, film, novel, animated movie, T-shirt, action figure, perfume, amusement park ride, and so on. In this article, I explore the relation between such media content and cross-media production. Furthermore, I critically discuss the implications for cultural theory and present a model of cross-media content transfer. The model shows what must be left behind in content–concept migrations across media, and presents the role and importance of games as a nexus in this exchange. I conclude that cross-media transfer happens relatively smoothly between forms that are alike, such as books and films, but less so between forms that have strong structural differences.

Today, the culture industries are not driven by storytelling, art, or visionary individuals. The Walt Disney era's focus on end-user experience has been replaced by the entertainment industry's need to minimize risk in the face of rising cost of production and advertising, which means that no stand-alone product, whether film, game, or even comic book is worth risking the investment. The risk has to be spread across media, and beyond, to secure the bottom line.

In this article some of the relations between media content and cross-media production is explored, with the focus on movies and games. In addition, implications for cultural theory are critically discussed. The main observation is that the medium no longer is the message (if it ever was). Instead, in the words of cross-media producers David Alpert and Rick Jacobs (2004), "Movies are now no longer free-standing IP [intellectual property]; they are one piece in a marketing assault." Or, as Jay Lemke (2004) put it, "Maximizing profits compels a strategy of crossing over across as many of these media as possible."

Correspondence should be addressed to Espen Aarseth, IT- University of Copenhagen, Rued Langgaardsvej 7, 2300 Copenhagen, Denmark. E-mail: aarseth@itu.dk

Today, risk-adverse producers and investors seek to capitalize on marketing by co-launching concepts through multiple media: the game, film, novel, animated movie, T-shirt, action figure, perfume, amusement park ride, and so on. Typical examples are the *Lord of the Rings* and the *Harry Potter* cross-productions. In addition, films such as *The Matrix* have been followed by a game and the animation film *Animatrix*. This has caught on to the extent that the *Chronicles of Riddick* game–film was accompanied by an animated DVD named on the package, ridiculously,[1] "Ani Riddick."

Another example of this is the concept–license "Death Jr." (Konami, 2005). Not a film; not a game; not a comic book; and not an action figure, but all of these and more.[2] As a Sony PlayStation Portable launch title, "Death Jr." is a prime example of how concept licenses, rather than content, move between media platforms. This article examines what implications this has for the types of message that can be reproduced.

Using Cawelti's (1976) theory of popular genres, the article presents a model of cross-media content transfer, showing what must be left behind in content–concept migrations across media, and the role and importance of games as a nexus in this exchange. Will games replace movies as the economical terminal platform (book–comic–film–game) or has game technology and the Hollywood-comparable cost of game production already redefined the cycle? Story, game, or sculpture? As such, we need to develop a critical language to address and analyze cross-media assets and their cultural cycles. The analysis presented in this article is focused on comparative studies of content. To gain a full perspective on the "poetics" of cross-media productions, however, this should be accompanied by a study of the cross-media industry: the economics of cross-media financing, licensing, marketing, and distribution.

TRANSFERRING "CONTENT": MIGRATION, FRANCHISE, BRANDING

"Content" is a tricky word. It usually signals the importance of something other than that to what it refers—often the container. Those who actually focus on the content—for example, a professor of literature or visual art, would never use the word to describe their object: the content of Shakespeare or the content of Botticelli. Rather, it is used when something other than the content is the main focus,

---

[1]The animated short film directed by Peter Chung (2004) was called *Dark Fury* (2004). The title "Ani Riddick" completely misses the elegant wordplay of the "Animatrix" title, but the logic of pre-awareness dictated an Animatrix-like name, to signal a similar relation between this product and the main films.

[2]http://www.deathjr.com/

such as the medium and its material, or technological, social, or political conditions. In this article, however, the focus is on the content-side of content, and not on the container aspect. However, the key question is whether content can be transferred between media so here, too, the term is mostly used negatively.

What is a *cross-media production*? There are two forms, synchronous and asynchronous, which we might also see as the "strong" and "weak" versions: Cross-media productions that produce the media versions in parallel, and productions that take place sequentially, as a migration between media, and where the first instance usually is seen as the original content. At some point the latter becomes merely an adaptation, in which a work is translated from one medium to another, without any plan for such transfer at the time of first creation. The distinction between adaptation and cross-media production can be difficult to maintain, however, as many works may have been made with cross-media migration in mind. Typically, low-cost media such as books afford a later transfer to high-cost media (movies) that often depends on, and is initiated by, the success of the initial product, whereas high-cost media products afford simultaneous transfers to low-cost media (e.g., novelizations and comic book versions). It should be pointed out that cross-media productions do not have to be entertainment, but could be documentary, journalistic, or didactic instead. However, the perspective in this article is limited to entertainment cross-media productions and properties that involve a game in their chain of output.

Historically, it is possible to trace cross-media productions back to antiquity, in which a play or poem in manuscript form, both intended to be performed and read, in principle could be seen as an early example. Similarly, 18th-century sheet music allowing upper-class families to recreate contemporary chamber music compositions in their homes might be seen as an early parallel to the music recording industry or the home VCR revolution of the early 80s.[3] This is not the place to give an account of the history of cross-media production, but it should be noted that the principle is old and covers many genres and types of content.

Before the advent of commercial games some three decades ago, movies were the normal terminal in the chain of cross-media migration. An intellectual property might start as a play, novel, or comic book, or even as a song or a painting, and would migrate up the cost chain and end up as a Hollywood movie. An obvious example is Tracy Chevalier's (1999) novel *Girl with a Pearl Earring,* based on Vermeer's 1665 painting, and turned into a movie directed by Peter Webber (2003), with Scarlett Johansson in the title role. Here we note how Vermeer's visual style bypasses a link in the chain and informs the movie directly.

Today, however, game productions are starting to rival movie productions in terms of cost and, therefore, the position on top of the cost chain. Movies and com-

---

[3] About the latter, see Wasser (2001).

puter games are now the most interesting cross-media pair, because in addition to being rather different in terms of cognitive and social affordances, their modes of production are more alike than most other output types. According to David Alpert and Rick Jacobs (2004), the average cost of a Hollywood film in 2003 was $63.8 million. In addition, another $39 million was used to market each movie, making the total $103 million. Game productions are still less costly on average, but they may start to reach comparable figures in the near future, as the "third generation consoles" (PlayStation 3, Xbox360, and Nintendo Wii) dramatically increase the need for animation labor due to the more demanding graphics resolutions and formats such as High Definition television.

As Alpert and Jacobs (2004) pointed out, movies increasingly are being remade from earlier versions or from other content sources. For example:

- Novels (*Harry Potter*)
- Comics (*Spider Man*)
- Games (*Tomb Raider, Doom*)
- Television shows (*Starsky and Hutch*)
- Earlier movies (*Italian Job*)
- Amusement park rides (*Pirates of the Caribbean*)

The reason for this, they claim, is that pre-awareness reduces risk, by making the marketing of the movie less costly and more effective. The same trend exists in the game industry in which most best selling titles are sequels, movie franchises, or often both. Given this financial logic, in which cost recovery is the core value of the operation, certain observations can be framed about the types of transformations afforded by the cross-media industry:

1. A single-medium launch is a lost opportunity, a flawed business plan.
2. The health and timeliness of the overall production and launch is more important than the integrity of an individual piece.
3. The individual pieces should add to the total franchise–brand awareness.
4. Ease of transfer (crossability) becomes a critical aspect of the operation.

Therefore, the somewhat romantic notion of cross-media content should be replaced with the more accurate term cross-media branding, which may include transfer of the content to a greater or lesser degree.

How is content transferred? Does it even have to be? The logic of advertising suggests that the logo is all you need to brand successfully (e.g., "Batman candy"). However, audience acceptance is also critical to the health of the brand, and the fulfillment of audience expectations clearly depends on medium conventions and affordances. In other words, producers cannot stray too far from audience expectations if they wish to keep the brand healthy. This was clearly seen in Tim Burton's risky lead casting of the comic actor Michael Keaton in the first *Batman* movie, which was met with significant prelaunch skepticism, especially among fans of the comic book. In that case the product was strong enough to succeed. However, a less-successful example may be found in the game *Enter the Matrix* (2003) in which the greatest disappointment may have been the simple fact that the audiences' expectations of a *Matrix* game franchise far exceeded the actual game's ability to outshine its competition. This may be especially because *Max Payne,* 2 years earlier, had implemented the "bullet time" effect of the first movie. Although *Enter the Matrix* made a profit, it was also the most-returned (to the store) game ever. Also, it did not get great reviews, which made the license owner, Warner Bros., unhappy enough to suggest that licensed games that did not receive good review ratings would be penalized by higher royalty fees, to prevent brand damage.

WHAT TRANSFERS?

Many examples are needed to fully investigate the aesthetic mechanisms of content transfer. In this article, relatively few are used, so the conclusions reached must remain tentative and in need of further verification. Clearly, a content migration from one medium to another depends on a number of factors, making each case special. However, some general observations can be made, even at the outset: Adaptations are not always successful. Financial success can sometimes be due to substantial marketing and pre-awareness, rather than high quality, but at the cost of possible brand damage. And because production companies have a fairly realistic sense of what will work, they select projects with the best chances for success. In the film-to-game business, it is easy to spot the pattern: Only certain types of film become games. Key words here are action, science fiction, horror, and war; in other words, spatial spectacle. Interestingly, games do not seem to afford the transfer of many genres that we recognize from book to film: romance, psychodrama, period–historical, or biography. Successful book-to-film transfers, such as *Remains of the Day* or comic book to film transfers such as *Ghostworld,* will never make the leap to game and for good reason: The narrative affinities and affordances shared by books and films are not shared by games. In other words, we are not witnessing cross-media storytelling, but rather cross-media spectacle making.

One interesting example is Walt Disney's last amusement park ride from Disneyland, *Pirates of the Caribbean* (1973). This is a boat ride through a spectacular series of tableaus, showing (among other things) grinning skeletons, mounds of gold and treasure, imprisoned pirates, a sea-to-land cannon battle, the sacking of a town, and pirates celebrating and singing the famous "Yo ho, yo ho! A pirate's life for me!" In time for its 30-year anniversary, Disney released a film (subtitled *The Curse of the Black Pearl*) and a game bearing the same title, but without a subtitle. Comparing these three works, however, reveals that there is almost nothing in common between any of them except the title and the brand logo. The characters of the film, Johnny Depp, Keira Knightley, and Orlando Bloom, do not figure in either the game or the ride. A few individual tableaus from the ride, such as the cannon battle and the jailed pirates trying to lure the keys from a dog, can be seen briefly in the film, but most of the tableaus are not transferred. The film tells a story of love, inheritance, and release from immortality—themes found neither in the ride or the game. In fact, the only element from the film found in the game is the voice of Keira Knightley, used as voiceover. This is understandable given the fact that the game was commissioned by Disney very late in the production process, and it was conceived independently as the follow-up to a strategy, role-playing game hybrid called *Sea Dogs* and was originally destined to become *Sea Dogs II*. More striking, then, is the lack of overlap between the ride and the film. Even rides with "narrative" content, such as the *Peter Pan* or *Winnie-the-Pooh* rides in Disneyland, or *The Mummy* or *Jurassic Park* rides at Universal Studios in Hollywood, do not recapture tellable story moments that would be associated with the books or the films of the same name. The rides depend on pre-awareness of the narrative, but offer nothing narrative in return. Amusement park rides, obviously, are not narratives, but obey other laws of presentation. To get a deeper perspective of this, let us turn to popular fiction theorist John Cawelti (1976), who made a distinction between two levels of popular fiction. He said the distinction is: (a) the level of cultural convention, in which we find the stereotypes, characters, clichés, and the environment (e.g., Europe in the Middle Ages, the Wild West) and (b) the level of the underlying structure, which is a series of events (boy meets girls, boy loses girl, etc.). Only the latter is where the story is actually told, but the amusement park rides and the games contain the first level without really affording the latter.

This can be seen even more clearly when we look at the transfers that actually work across the story–game frontier. Book–film–game transfers do exist, and perhaps the best examples here are the *Lord of the Rings* and *Harry Potter* franchises. If we study these carefully, we see that all elements that transfer between book and film may not travel all the way to the game. The actual events of the books are usually transferred reasonably faithfully to the films, except where length dictates that elements may be removed to shorten the viewing time. In the games, however, the story lines from the books–films are not recapitulated faithfully, if at all.

Again, Cawelti's (1976) model applies, with the layer of cultural conventions being transferred, but the underlying narrative structure not at all or bent almost out of recognition. Playing Gandalf in the Electronic Arts *Return of the King* (2003) game involves zapping orcs (i.e., evil creatures) endlessly and performing ninja-like moves with sword and staff, but with none of the inventiveness and dignity that the narrative Gandalf would have displayed. Are we playing Gandalf, or merely a Gandalf-like puppet? On the other hand, one would also have hoped that the rich, beautiful world of middle earth would have been more freely explorable in the game, but instead we are served a very linear action corridor, a unicursal labyrinth that offers as much individual choice as a train ride.

Harry Potter games such as the *Chamber of Secrets* (2002) are more openly explorable, because one can wander around Hogwarts and explore in a multicursal fashion, but here also the transfer of narrative events from the book are nowhere as faithful as in the movie. Furthermore, the main game event elements, such as collecting jellybeans and fighting various monsters, are not derived from the narrative works, and correspond to nothing in them. Again, Cawelti (1976) can be used to describe a transfer that, similar to chemical warfare, kills the people (or turns them into brainless zombies) but leaves the buildings untouched.

A possible alternative to the sequential media migration can be found in the cross-media franchise, "Death Jr." "Death Jr." is not a movie, comic book, game, T-shirt, action figure, belt-buckle, or piece of jewelry but is, rather, all of these things. "Death Jr." started life as a game engine demo,[4] and was soon licensed for several simultaneous media productions. Even before any audience had gotten to know this new phenomenon, it made money on cross-licensing rights. The idea behind "Death Jr." is very simple: He is just a normal kid going to school, but with a very special father, the grim reaper. "Death Jr." is the logical offspring of cross-media productions and one that offers a flexibility of freedom that already established franchises cannot match, but in terms of pre-awareness, it is still quite a risk. "Death Jr." offers an alternative model to the other examples in this article, which should throw new light on the evolution of the culture industry into the age of cross-media. Unfortunately, the Sony PlayStation Portable game, launched in August 2005, was not a success so the future for the "Death Jr." franchise looks a bit grim at the time of writing.

LOST IN TRANSLATION

According to Alpert and Jacobs (2004), there are three things to look for in the evaluation of a possible film-to-game transfer: (a) Iconic characters with high recognition value, (b) an interesting universe, and (c) a "high concept" that would translate into a game play mechanic. If you have all three, you may be able to make an interesting game, but it is still difficult. What is lacking from this formula, of course, is story. Partly because you do not really need it, if you have these key ingredients, and partly because, as the *Lord of the Rings* and *Harry Potter* examples have shown, you cannot really use it anyway. You can transfer characters (up to a

---

[4]A *game engine* is a simple game that demonstrates the virtues of a new graphics engine for a game software platform.

Element	Ride to Movie	Book to movie	Movie to game	Game to movie
Storyline	No	Ok	Not really	No
Events	Hardly	Ok	Hardly	Ok
Universe	Ok	Ok	Ok	Ok
Character	No	Ok	Partly	Expanded

FIGURE 1   Cross-media transfer table.

point), universes (non-problematically), and any kind of action gimmick such as bullet time; but for games to work, game play (and not story) is key. A predefined story will mess up the game if followed too slavishly. Therefore the method is to extract the spectacular, the spatial and the idiosyncratic, and develop events and way points that will nod to the story of the original work, whereas keeping a firm eye on the bottom line of game play quality.

Previous commentators on cross-media (e.g., Jenkins, 2003; Klastrup & Tosca, 2004) pointed out that "world" is a key transferable element, especially when it comes to game transfers. I prefer to use the more open word "universe," as it allows for the possibility of only a rudimentary compatibility between the content of two productions. However, even here, the term is a metaphor at best. There is no "world" or "universe" as such being transferred between media platforms—only partial and more or less faithfully represented elements. The orcs and elves of Blizzard's *Warcraft* universe are clearly not identical to the orcs and elves of Tolkien's middle earth. Thus, Cawelti's (1976) idea of a cultural convention seems more appropriate when describing the kinship between the various Tolkien-derived (and semi-derived) universes, or even between the universes by a single creator, such as Richard Garriott's various *Ultima* games.

CONCLUSION

This preliminary study shows that cross-media transfer happens relatively smoothly between forms that are alike, such as books and films, and less so between forms that have strong structural differences, such as amusement park rides, games, and narratives. There may be examples that contradict this or tell a different story, but the economically grounded practice of the entertainment industry gives a good indication of what is, and what is not, viable. Cawelti's (1976) model provides a very relevant indicator of what can and cannot be translated easily. It is also a good way to get past the confusing notion of storytelling, and instead focus on and attempt to understand, universe building, character construction, and the translation of concepts into media-specific mechanisms. This way, we can also begin to see what traditional authors have been doing when they construct the universes they use to grow their narratives.

Cross-media productions come in many shapes and depend on a large number of arts: storytelling, game design, and concept development among them. But a good sense for business may be the most important one. To understand this market-driven logic, the research strategy seems simple enough: Follow the money!

REFERENCES

Alpert, D., & Jacobs, R. (2004, October). *Videogames & licensing in the Hollywood film market.* Presentation at the Korea Games Conference, Seoul, Korea.
Bartkowiak, A. (Director). (2005). *Doom* [Motion picture]. United States: Universal Pictures
Burton, T. (Director). (1989). *Batman* [Motion picture]. United States: Warner Brothers.
Cawelti, J. (1976). *Adventure, mystery, and romance: Formula stories as art and popular culture.* Chicago: The University of Chicago Press.
Chevalier, T. (1999). *Girl with a pearl earring.* London: HarperCollins.
Chung, P. (Director). (2004). dark fury. United States: Universal Pictures.
EA Pacific (dev.) (2003). Return of the King [Software]. United States: Electronic Arts.
EA Redwood Shores Studio (dev.) (2002) Harry Potter and the chamber of secrets [Software]. United States: Electronic Arts.
Gray, F. G. (Director). (2003) *The Italian job* [Motion picture]. United States: Paramount Pictures.
Jenkins, H. (2003, January). Transmedia storytelling. *Technology Review.* Boston: MIT Press. Retrieved January 24, 2006, from http://www.technologyreview.com/articles/03/01/wo_jenkins011503.asp?p=1)
Klastrup, L., & Tosca, S. (2004). Transmedial worlds: Rethinking cyberworld design. *Proceedings, International Conference on Cyberworlds 2004.* Los Alamitos, CA: IEEE Computer Society. Retrieved January 24, 2006, from http://www.itu.dk/people/klastrup/klastruptosca_transworlds.pdf
Konami. (2005). Death, Jr. Retrieved July 18, 2006, from http://www.deathjr.com
Lemke, J. (2004). *Critical analysis across media: Games, franchises, and the new cultural order.* Presented at the First International Conference on Critical Discourse Analysis, Valencia, Spain. Retrieved July 18, 2006, from http://www.personal.umich.edu/~jaylemke/papers/Franchises/Valencia-CDA-Franchises.htm
Phillips, T. (Director). (2004) *Starsky and Hutch* [Motion picture]. United States: Warner Brothers.
Raimi, S. (Director).(2002). *Spider Man: The motion picture* [Motion picture]. United States: Columbia Pictures.
Verbinski, G. (Director). (2003). *Pirates of the caribbean: Curse of the black pearl* [Motion picture]. United States: Walt Disney Pictures.
Wachowski Andy and Larry Wachowski (Writer/Directors). (1999) *The Matrix* [Motion picture]. United States: Warner Brothers
Wasser, F. (2001). *Veni, vidi, video: The Hollywood empire and the VCR.* Austin: University of Texas Press.
Webber, P. (Director). (2003). *Girl with pearl earring* [Motion picture]. United States: Lions Gate Films.
West, S. (Director).(2001). *Lara Croft: Tomb raider* [Motion picture]. United States: Paramount Pictures.

POPULAR COMMUNICATION, 4(3), 213–224

Reality Play: Documentary Computer Games Beyond Fact and Fiction

Joost Raessens

Utrecht University

Computer games such as *JFK Reloaded* and *9-11 Survivor* not only aim at an accurate documentation of particular events—such as the assassination of John F. Kennedy and the Twin Towers attack—but also at the playful re-enactment of these traumatic events. In this article, I discuss whether the phrase "documentary computer games" is useful in defining these games. These "docu-games" try to combine the facts of documentaries and the fiction of computer games—elements that seem hard to reconcile at first sight. Do these games create a harmonious "space of communication" in which feelings of mutual understanding occur between designers and players?

Truth is never easily come by. Like Don Quixote, we can be perplexed by the intertwining of the credible and the fantastic.

Rodney Bolt, *History Play*

Exactly 41 years after John F. Kennedy (JFK) was assassinated in Dallas in 1963, the Scottish company Traffic Games released the computer game *JFK Reloaded* on November 22, 2004.[1] The objective of the game is to enable players to adopt the position of Lee Harvey Oswald, killing JFK with three bullets. Players earn points if they succeed in matching their shots with the official version of the events as described by the Warren Commission. Established by Lyndon B. Johnson, the Warren Commission investigated the assassination, and in 1964 presented its *single bullet* theory, or, as conspiracy theorists prefer to call it, the *magic bullet* theory. According to this theory, a single bullet fired by Oswald caused seven injuries to

Correspondence should be addressed to Joost Raessens, Faculty of Arts, Institute for Media and Re/presentation, Utrecht University, Kromme Nieuwegracht 29, 3512 HD Utrecht, The Netherlands. E-mail: joost.raessens@let.uu.nl

[1]I use the term "computer games" broadly and do not distinguish between the different available platforms.

the bodies of JFK and Governor John Connally from Texas—even for experienced players certainly not an easy task to perform.

Although the Kennedy family apparently called the game "despicable," the developers defended *JFK Reloaded* by arguing that those players who succeeded in realizing the goal of the game reinforced the truth of the most important conclusion of the Warren Commission: There was no conspiracy, and Oswald acted alone. This lone gunman theory contradicts approximately 75% of Americans whose opinions were strengthened by Oliver Stone's movie, *JFK* (1991), in their conviction that some kind of conspiracy existed. According to the director of Traffic Games, Kirk Ewing (n.d.), *JFK Reloaded* wrote "documentary history" by using game technology to enable people to reenact the assassination in an interactive way. This educational docu-game, as Traffic Games characterized it, is said to combine elements of the documentary and the computer game by enabling the player to recreate this historical event in an interactive way, without the spectacle and the fiction of Stone's movie.[2]

When analyzing the ways in which players discussed this game on the Water Cooler Games forum, three types of reactions can be discerned.[3] The players who stated that the assassination of JFK "has been such a big historical controversy, a simulation seems like an instructive way to understand it," surrender to the simulation by taking it at interface value. On the other hand, those players who stated, "it seems ridiculous that a simulation could concretely prove anything" and discharge the game as "some programmers using an event in history to make some cash," are denying the game's importance. Players who argued, "the developers claim they believe Oswald acted alone, they built the game to favour this assumption," are discussing the game's built-in assumptions. Although several commentators criticized Traffic Games for "selling" the game as an educational aide only, the discussion shows that users appropriated this commercial game for what Turkle (1996) called "consciousness-raising" (p. 71).

---

[2]On the Water Cooler Games forum, Ian Bogost described this game as follows: "It's very ... antiseptic, let's say, very scientific. There is little attempt to create a sense of reward or pleasure in the violence. The player is very focused on the ballistics and the timing" (see www.watercoolergames.org/archives/000295.shtml).

[3]These reactions resemble the three possible answers Sherry Turkle (1996) had to "the seduction of simulation" (p. 71). According to Turkle, players can surrender to the seduction (simulation resignation), reject it (simulation denial), or learn to deconstruct the assumptions that are built into the simulation (simulation understanding). This last option is the one Turkle seemed to favor. The game was distributed via www.jfkreloaded.com. These reactions can be found at the forum of Water Cooler Games (see Note 2). Although *JFK Reloaded* is a simulation with persuasive motives, it contains textual and contextual indications that we must switch to what Roger Odin (1995b) called "a documentarizing lecture" (p. 234). Computer game-based political messaging as *Tax Invaders* (see the article by Ian Bogost, this issue), does not contain these kinds of indications.

DOCUMENTARY COMPUTER GAMES

Contemporary computer games not only simulate events from which people have a certain distance, such as the assassination of JFK, but also more recent events for which precise impact is hard to decipher now, such as the attack on the Twin Towers. They are called "documentary computer games" because they attempt to document such traumatic events in a historically correct way as well as playfully reenacting them. These docu-games are part of so-called serious games, games used in areas such as education, training, and politics that go beyond mere entertainment purposes. Because these games are in different degrees based on actual news events, they also may be referred to as "news gaming."[4] In this article I investigate to what extent and in which ways computer games can be viewed as a documentary medium.[5]

In most cases, documentary computer games are developed by collectives of game developers, artists, and political activists who use games to foreground social and political issues. Computer game technology offers a new generation of artists accessible tools to either entirely create new games from scratch or develop modifications of existing commercial releases—turning a platform for pure fantasy into a medium for social realism and critique.[6] Whether the commercial game industry is focused on the production of fictional worlds (e.g., *Grand Theft Auto* [Rockstar Games, 2004] and *The Sims* [Electronic Arts, 2000]) or on realistic reconstructions of real life (think of sports games, e.g., *FIFA 06* [Electronic Arts, 2006]), the pursuit of historical accuracy is explicitly subservient to entertainment value. Docu-games on the other hand, strive for "facticity" or "documentarity" to expose players to events and places that would remain inaccessible to them otherwise.[7]

Mainstream games, such as *Grand Theft Auto* and *FIFA 06,* are based on fictional or realistic scenarios in which the intensity of feeling and the reflexivity of

---

[4]See www.newsgaming.com. Gonzalo Frasca's own games *Madrid* and *September 12th* deal with the 3/11 terrorist attacks in Spain and the War on Terror. Other games in this category are *9-11 Survivor, Waco Resurrection,* and *Escape from Woomera*—games I discuss in this article. *Kuma\War* is referred to as a "reality game" that offers "playable re-creations of real war events released weeks after they occur" (see www.kumawar.com).

[5]On November 30th, 2005, the International Documentary Festival Amsterdam in cooperation with Mediamatic (www.mediamatic.nl), organized an evening program about computer games as a documentary medium. Speakers were Brody Condon, Julian Oliver, Michael Lew, and myself. For more information, see www.idfa.com.

[6]The questions I raise in this article are related to those of Alexander R. Galloway (2004) and Gonzalo Frasca (2004) who analyzed the possibilities of computer games to deal with social realism (Galloway) and social and political issues (Frasca). Although Galloway took traditional theories of realism as his point of departure, Frasca's explorations were mainly based on the work of drama theorist Augusto Boal. My own perspective is that of the discourse on documentary.

[7]To fall within my definition of a documentary game, simulations have to contain textual and contextual indications that we must switch to a "documentarizing lecture," such as the actual events the games I

thought are, in the end, subordinated to the actuality and causality of action (Kattenbelt & Raessens, 2003). Docu-games, on the other hand, try to break through the dominance of action to do justice to the complexity of experience: feeling, reflexivity, and action in their mutual relation. As I explain more in detail next, special attention is paid to the intensity of feeling in *9-11 Survivor* (Kinematic, 2003), and to reflection and critical thinking in *Escape from Woomera* (2003). The fact that these docu-games immerse players in the reality of the game while offering them all kinds of possibilities to participate (see Raessens, 2005), for example in making choices with moral implications, transforms play into a meaningful, interactive experience.

Before engaging in the theoretical discussion about the documentary status of computer games in more detail, I present three further examples of computer games that are considered documentaries in one way or another.[8]

9-11 Survivor (2003)

One of the artists involved in the development of docu-games is Brody Condon, who also teaches game design in Los Angeles. Condon supervised the game design class that produced *9-11 Survivor* and was a member of the art collective C-level from Los Angeles that was responsible for the production of *Endgames: Waco Resurrection* (C-level, 2003).

In *9-11 Survivor,* which was briefly available on the Internet in 2003, the player is trapped in the burning Twin Towers on September 11, 2001. In one scenario the player is a businessman unable to find an escape route. The only choice the player has is to perish by fire or plunge to death. In other scenarios, the player is able to escape because he or she is situated on one of the lower floors of the building, he or she has a gas mask available, or a few brave firefighters come to the rescue.

The three students, John Brennan, Mike Caloud, and Jeff Cole, who formed the art collective Kinematic that was responsible for this game, received death threats and were publicly condemned for bad taste and moral indecency. They were accused of exploiting this tragedy commercially. However, it was never their intention to release a commercial version of this game, and therefore, this accusation

---

discuss in this article are based on. As Odin (1995b) wrote, "a documentary will have a higher degree of 'documentarity'" (p. 229) the more it blocks operations that constitute the process of fictionalization. In *JFK Reloaded,* for example, the freedom to produce a story is blocked to a large degree. Being a docu-game, it would be impossible for Oswald not to aim at killing JFK. Games such as *The Sims* and *Food Force,* which are based on more abstract (but nonfantastic) events, do not block the production of a story in this way. Furthermore, the fact that the Food Force Web site (www.food-force.com) differentiates between "the game" and "the reality" is a contextual indication that favors a "fictionalizing" lecture of the game over a "documentarizing" one.

[8]For more information on the work of Brody Condon, see www.tmpspace.com. For information on *9-11 Survivor,* see www.selectparks.net/911survivor. For information on *Escape from Woomera,* see www.escapefromwoomera.org.

seems an untenable one. The goal of the game was to immerse the player in the terrifying surroundings of the burning towers and to let him or her experience how it must have felt to be trapped inside. The interactivity of the game, and the realistic nature of the design of the Twin Towers, enabled them to emphasize the immediacy of this frightening moment. This kind of immediacy was lost in the desensitization produced by the constant repetition of these images at CNN. A few months after its release, Kinematic withdrew the game from the Internet—not because of its controversial reception, but because the collective received an $8,000 bill for heavy site traffic.

Endgames: Waco Resurrection (2003)

This game from C-level is a reality-based, role-playing game in which four players assume the role of the cult leader David Koresh at his virtually reconstructed compound in Waco, TX. Koresh, head of a religious sect called the Branch Davidians, was killed when the FBI burst into his compound on February 29th, 1993—an attack that took the lives of 85 members of the sect. According to C-level, this game is an interactive documentary that pays much attention to historic details. The designers of the game used authentic images made during the attack and sound recordings of David Koresh himself.

The players wear hard plastic masks with built-in microphones that function as interface. Assuming the role of Koresh, the four players run around the compound, shooting at FBI agents and other opponents. The game was released in 2003, which was 10 years after the event. According to C-Level, Koresh is the paradoxical personification of the political landscape of the United States: He is both the besieged and assaulted "other" as well as a logical continuation of the neo-conservative political vision. Players experience this paradoxical situation when adopting the role of Koresh.

Escape from Woomera (2003)

In 1998 Julian Oliver founded Selectparks, a collective of game developers, artists, and political activists, in Melbourne, Australia. This collective used games as a political, documentary medium. In *Escape from Woomera,* designed by Julian Oliver and two of his friends, players are invited to adopt the character of an asylum seeker who is imprisoned in an immigration detention center while his application for asylum is under consideration. By immersing themselves interactively in this world, which otherwise would be completely hidden from view, and living through the experiences, gamers gain an insight into the miserable living conditions of these asylum seekers. Players are challenged to escape by using the means available to them, such as digging tunnels, scaling fences, or using the legal help of sympathetic lawyers.

The designers of *Escape from Woomera* also received a hostile reception for using the medium of the computer game for a serious discussion of a human rights issue in Australia. They based their game on extensive documentary research, revealing that the Australian government had been withholding information about the inhuman conditions of immigration detention centers such as Woomera. Remarkably enough, the game was co-financed by the Australia Council for the Arts. Phillip Ruddock, then Immigration Minister, was not amused by this contribution of $25,000 (Australian) to a game that in his opinion pushed players into what he called "unlawful behavior." The Woomera Detention Center was closed in April 2003.

FACT OR FICTION?

The creators of the computer games mentioned previously claim that they are documentary, but at first sight this claim seems far from convincing. The arguments that have been used to criticize the documentary film (see Kessler, 1998) also seem to apply to the medium of the computer game.

According to the first of these three arguments, the documentary can never live up to its traditional claim of representing reality objectively. As Michael Renov (1993a) argued, "nonfiction contains any number of 'fictive' elements, moments at which a presumably objective representation of the world encounters the necessity of creative intervention" (p. 2). Due to the presence of the movie camera, which influences the filmed object, and through the use of framing, editing, narration, musical accompaniment, characters, and voiceover, a documentary creates its own object and by doing so, its own "truth." As a discursive form, documentary "*constitutes* the objects which it pretends only to describe realistically and to analyze objectively" (Renov, 1993a, p. 7). When applying this argument to so-called documentary computer games, we have to conclude that even when these games succeed in being more or less historically accurate, they always occupy a comparable tense position between fact and fiction.[9]

The second argument is concerned with the possibilities of digital manipulation. The arrival of the digital image has seriously undermined the idea that the photographic image, considered to be an indexical sign, has the status of scientific evidence. The discourse of photography has traditionally been called on to legitimatize the documentary film; hence, the reduction of the indexical status of the photographic image causes the documentary to lose its legitimization. When comparing the views of two authors who have been crucial in this debate, we immedi-

---

[9]As Renov (1993a) wrote, "the common bonds between fiction and nonfiction may be illuminated with concepts drawn from historiography, postmodernist theory, and philosophy" (p. 4). Referring to the work of the Italian postmodern philosopher Gianni Vattimo, I further elaborate on this issue in Raessens (2005).

ately grasp the impact of the process of digitization. On one hand, in his work, "The Ontology of the Photographic Image," André Bazin (1967) defined the photographic image as follows: "The photographic image is the object itself, the object freed from the conditions of time and space that govern it" (p. 14). Brian Winston (1993), on the other hand, defined the impact of digital retouching technology as follows: "In the longer term, this leaves the documentary film project in all its guises in parlous state" (p. 56). Two years later, he wrote: "These technological developments ... will have a profound and perhaps fatal impact on the documentary film. It is not hard to imagine that every documentarist will shortly (that is, in the next fifty years) have to hand, in the form of a desktop personal video-image-manipulating computer, the wherewithal for complete fakery. What can or will be left of the relationship between image and reality?" (p. 6). Because computer games are at best simulations of reality, as they are not composed of photochemically produced images but of computer generated images, they would hence lack every kind of legitimization to a documentary status.

The third argument is not from media theory, but from traditional historical theory. Historians who are inspired by the 19th century German historian Leopold von Ranke think that the writing of history comes down to saying "what really happened." They "see their profession as objective, accretive, and teleologically governed as each generation of scholarship refines the truth and attributes additional data" (Uricchio, 2005, p. 336). Their basic assumption—that there are stable, fixed historical facts that the historian reveals—is inconsistent with one of the most distinguishing characteristics of computer games: interactivity. As William Uricchio argued, "the interaction between a present-day player and the representation of a historically specific world seems to challenge any notion of a unique configuration of historical 'fact' and 'fixity,' giving way instead to the historically inconsistent and ludic" (p. 327). Thanks to interactivity, players are in the position to organize their own text in a playful manner and thereby construct their own meanings of the game.

DOCUMENTATION

On the basis of these three arguments, we might be tempted to conclude that computer games cannot be used for historical documentation.[10] However, these three arguments are themselves open to criticism.

As for the first argument, the documentary was never exclusively seen as a reproduction of objective reality resulting automatically from the very nature of the

---

[10]According to Noël Carroll (1996), these arguments against the non-fiction film are a form of postmodernist skepticism. He wanted to refute what he took to be "overly facile skepticism about the possibility of making motion pictures that are genuinely in the service of knowledge" (p. 285).

cinematographic apparatus. When the father of modern documentary, John Grierson, used the term "documentary" in the mid-20s to label the non-fiction films made by Robert J. Flaherty (e.g., *Nanook of the North*, 1922, and *Moana*, 1926), he stated that the documentary must be seen as a "creative treatment of actuality."[11] Even though this formulation lacks clarity about the specific relation between the actuality part—as a form of evidence—and the creative treatment part—as a form of manipulation—it does make clear that the documentary form is, as Renov pointed (1993a) out, "the more or less artful reshaping of the historical world" (p. 11). Because the computer games mentioned previously treat actuality in a creative way, Griersons' paradoxical definition allows us to consider these games as a form of documentary.

The second argument also is open to an important objection. There has been a shift in focus in the field of documentary theory in the 1980s. In describing documentary films, we no longer focus exclusively or primarily on the defining characteristics of the documentary image; for example, its indexical status.[12] The semio-pragmatic dimension of documentary film has become far more important, referring to the ways in which spectators or users are part of the structure and meaning of films that they treat as documentaries. According to the French semio- pragmatist Roger Odin (1995b, p. 234), individual spectators are able to produce a "documentarizing lecture" of each film—even a fictional film. If I watch, for example, Hitchcock's (1958) *Vertigo* because I wish to find out which hotel room is Judy Barton's (Kim Novak) at the moment Scottie (James Stewart) discovers her— because I am a Hitchcock fan wishing to rent this room for a night[13]—I exchange a "fictionalizing" lecture for a "documentarizing" one, even for a brief moment. According to Odin, films that we usually call "documentary" do not only contain textual but also contextual information that indicates that we must switch to such a documentarizing lecture.[14] Scientific animation films such as the BBC documentary *Walking with Dinosaurs* (broad-

---

[11]For the history of the word "documentary," see Winston (1995, pp. 11–14). According to the Internet Movie Database (http://www.amazon.imdb.com/title/tt0017162/trivia), "the word 'documentary' was first applied to films of this nature in an anonymous review of the movie [*Moana*] written by John Grierson, a.k.a. 'The Moviegoer,' in New York Sun, 8 February 1926."

[12]Galloway (2004) asked the same question: "Is social realism even possible in the medium of the videogame where each pixel is artificially created by the machine?" From the semio-pragmatic perspective I present in this article, it is possible to answer this question affirmatively.

[13]It is Room 401 of the York Hotel, San Francisco. In *Vertigo: The Making of a Hitchcock Classic* Dan Auiler (1998) referred incorrectly to Room 501—probably because the York Hotel promotes this room as the *Vertigo Room*.

[14]According to Odin (1995a), "any reading of an image consists of 'applying' to it processes that are essentially external to it. This reading does not result from an internal constraint, but from a cultural constraint" (p. 213). The fact that the International Documentary Festival Amsterdam organized a program about documentary computer games (see Footnote 5) can, for example, be considered as such a cultural constraint. Participants in this program are more likely to give a documentarizing lecture than those who play the games in another context.

cast in 1999) also may initiate such a documentarizing lecture.[15] The games mentioned previously contain historically accurate images in which the status as documentaries is explicitly established in a specific cultural space; that is on the accompanying Web sites and in interviews. Thus, they contain textual and contextual instructions that stimulate such a documentarizing lecture.[16]

Finally, the third argument equally invites criticism. The Rankean idea that writing history is saying "what really happened" can be situated at one of the extreme ends of the spectrum of historical theory. At the other end of the spectrum, we find poststructuralist historiography, "charged by its critics with upsetting the applecart of the historical trade by challenging notions of facticity, explanatory hierarchies, master narratives, and … the interpretative authority of the historian" (Uricchio, 2005, pp. 327–328). These historians argued that historical representations can never be "objective" but always will be present-day reconstructions. What traditional historians have called "objective" must be brought up for discussion. In addition, we need to put into question so-called authorities who claim the exclusive right to say what really happened. The computer games mentioned previously problematize the notions of "objectivity" and "authority," either to challenge them (CNN, Minister of Immigration) or to support them (Warren Rapport).

SUBLIME HISTORICAL EXPERIENCE

My affirmative answer, to the question of whether computer games can be considered documentary, is a dual one. I distinguish my argument from the pseudo-objectivity of the documentary as the representation of reality, and from the pseudo-subjectivity of its critics. When considering the arguments and counter-arguments mentioned here, I argue that documentary computer games are situated somewhere between both ends of the spectrum: They do not represent the historical reality objectively, but they are more than just subjective impressions of the artists involved.

For a better explanation of this specific position, I would like to turn briefly to a concept of the Dutch historian Frank Ankersmit (2005): the sublime historical experience. According to Ankersmit, both ends of the spectrum described here are disappointing because in their own way each of them excludes the notion of experience: "If you dispense with experience, you lack the intuition, openness and sus-

---

[15]The BBC (n.d.) Web site described *Walking with Dinosaurs* as follows: "Broadcast in 1999, *Walking with Dinosaurs* set out to create the most accurate portrayal of prehistoric animals ever seen on the screen. Combining fact and informed speculation with cutting-edge computer graphics and animatronics effects, the series took two years to make" (http://www.bbc.co.uk/sn/prehistoric_life/tv_radio/ wwdinosaurs).

[16]It would be interesting to analyze the different forms of realism in gaming for their ability to function as indications of a switch to a documentarizing lecture. Galloway (2004) distinguished realistic narrative (*The Sims*), realistic representation (*SOCOM Navy Seals* [Zipper Interactive, 2002]), and social realism (*Special Force* [Hizbullah Central Internet Bureau, 2003] and *Under Ash* [Dar Al-Fikr, 2001]).

ceptibility towards the knowable and, therefore, towards the past. That is the reason for my rehabilitation of experience as a source of insight" (as cited in Panhuysen, 2005, p. 43). Ankersmit connected the sublime experience with the experience of rupture, with dramatic events that cause changes: "These are the moments when present and past separate and the past is born as it were. 'The sublime' refers to the original meaning of the word when the pleasant and the terrible occur simultaneously" (Panhuysen, 2005, p. 43, author's translation).

The idea of the historical sublime seems to increase our understanding of what users experience when they play computer games such as *JFK Reloaded* and *9-11 Survivor* that simulate traumatic events in U.S. history. In both games, players reenact experiences of rupture that separated the past and present in a traumatic way. These experiences are paradoxical in a sublime way in the sense that they, as experiences that transcend the individual level,[17] involve and unite both the loss and pain of the trauma and, at the same time, the satisfaction of overcoming these feelings in terms of precognitive historical insights. This, however, does not free us from the question of whether these specific games are adequate stand-ins for lived experience. When it comes to the games described in this article no agreement has been reached on this point, as I have shown.

PLEA IN FAVOR OF THE DOCUMENTARY GAME

The four games I discuss in this article contain textual or contextual signs (or both) that justify a documentarizing lecture defining them as docu-games. When Renov (1993b) concluded that "It becomes very clear in the examination of the documentary film that the formal characteristics that define the cycles or styles of this film form (the actualité, cinépoem, or cinema vérité) are historically and ideologically contingent" (p. 19), there seems to be no reason to exclude games *a priori* from the category of the documentary form. This point of view makes even more sense when we take the poetics of the documentary into account. Renov described them as, "the four fundamental tendencies or rhetorical/aesthetic functions attributable to documentary practice ... 1. to record, reveal, or preserve; 2. to persuade or promote; 3. to analyze or interrogate; 4. to express" (p. 21). These four discursive functions are, indeed, present in the games I discuss here, albeit in different forms: the preservation of the traumatic experience in *9-11 Survivor*, the persuasion of the players of the inhuman conditions of immigration-detention centers in *Escape from Woomera*, the analysis of the assassination in *JFK Reloaded*, and the expression of the paradoxical position of David Koresh in *Waco Resurrection*.

---

[17]Henry Jenkins (2005) described computer games as "lively" works of art and as such these docu-games present players with the opportunity to experience something essential. Or in the words of the Dutch philosopher Henk Oosterling (2000), "The examples given are neither empirical evidence nor mere illustrations. They are—and here I am referring to Kant— exemplary ... Their exemplary quality makes them *singular-universal*" (p. 15, author's translation).

When looking at the issues gamers have brought up for discussion, for example on the Water Cooler Games forum, it struck me that they asked fundamental questions about the reliability of historical representation (*JFK*, the movie), simulation (*JFK*, the game), official information (e.g., the Warren Rapport), and details about detention centers (e.g., Woomera). When Renov (1993b) referred to the "impoverishment of a *documentary film culture*" (p. 20), games may offer what Renov was looking for; namely, "an energized climate of ideas and creative activities fueled by debate and public participation" (p. 20). Documentary computer games are capable of opening the area of the historical documentary to a large audience and may become very popular judging from the enthusiasm with which computer games generally are played and discussed. Whereas the documentary film has always tried to find stylistic as well as narrative ways to address spectators, gamers are immersed into experience and reenact historical events in interactive ways. Games are not only attractive because they please their users, but they could also turn out to be very effective in achieving such an educational effect.

If we prefer documentary computer games to really function in this way, designers have to pay attention to what Odin (1995b) called role adoption in the context of documentary films. A harmonious "space of communication" is only created if designer and player of the game adopt the same role, or as Odin called it "the same way of producing meaning and affects" (p. 227). Because the dominant communication regime in computer games is the "fictionalizing regime" (Odin, 1995b, p. 228), as is the case with film, documentary games run the same risk as documentary films; namely, of being "something we hardly have the desire to look at spontaneously, since it is often regarded as something that is fundamentally boring" (Odin, 1995b, p. 230).[18] The public will only accept the documentary computer game if it creates something that could be described by the neologism "faction": the combination of "facticity" or "documentarity" with the pleasure derived from playing fictional computer games. One of the biggest challenges of game design is precisely this difficult task to create *satis-faction*: to harmoniously include "this documentarizing communication pact" into computer games and thereby go beyond fact and fiction.

ACKNOWLEDGMENTS

This article is written within the Utrecht Media Research program (see www.let.uu.nl/umr). I thank Frank Kessler for helpful comments on this article.

---

[18]On the Water Cooler Game forum, *JFK Reloaded* was criticized by one of the players for this reason: "I couldn't consider this a game unless you could improve upon or alter the events in any way, aside from timing, such as moving to a different position, or somehow creating a new chain of events. If I went to the store and bought a game only to find out I can do nothing but aim my gun and shoot 3 bullets in the same scenario over and over, I'd return it immediately ... that's not a game." In this case it is obvious that the space of communication was not created harmoniously.

REFERENCES

Ankersmit, F. (2005). *Sublime historical experience*. Palo Alto, CA: Stanford University Press.

Auiler, D. (1998). *Vertigo: The making of a Hitchcock classic*. New York: St. Martin's Press.

Bazin, A. (1967). The ontology of the photographic image. In A. Bazin (Ed.), *What is cinema?* (pp. 9–16). Berkeley: University of California Press.

BBC. (n.d.). *Walking with dinosaurs*. Retrieved January 23, 2006, from http://www.bbc.co.uk/sn/prehistoric_life/tv_radio/wwdinosaurs/

Bolt, R. (2005). *History play*. London: Harper Perennial.

Carroll, N. (1996). Nonfiction film and postmodernist skepticism. In D. Bordwell & N. Carroll (Eds.), *Post-theory: Reconstructing film studies* (pp. 283–306). Madison: The University of Wisconsin Press.

Ewing, K. (n.d.). *JFK reloaded*. Retrieved January 23, 2006, from http://www.jfkreloaded.com/

Frasca, G. (2004). Videogames of the oppressed: Critical thinking, education, tolerance, and other trivial issues. In N. Wardrip-Fruin & P. Harrigan (Eds.), *Firstperson: New media as story, performance, and game* (pp. 85–94). Cambridge, MA: MIT Press.

Galloway, A. R. (2004). Social realism in gaming. *Game Studies: The International Journal of Computer Game Research, 4*(1). Retrieved from http://www.gamestudies.org.

Jenkins, H. (2005). Games, the new lively art. In J. Raessens & J. Goldstein (Eds.), *Handbook of computer game studies* (pp. 175–192). Cambridge, MA: MIT Press.

Kattenbelt, C., & Raessens, J. (2003). Computer games and the complexity of experience. In M. Copier & J. Raessens (Eds.), *Level up: Digital games research conference* (pp. 420–425). Utrecht: Faculty of Arts, Utrecht University.

Kessler, F. (1998). Fakt oder fiktion? Zum pragmatischen Status dokumentarischer bilder [Fact or fiction? On the pragmatic status of documentary images]. In *Montage/AV, 7/2/1998* (pp. 63–78). Marburg, Germany: Schüren Verlag.

Stone, O. (Director). (1991). *JFK* [Motion picture]. United States: Warner Brothers.

Odin, R. (1995a). For a semio-pragmatics of film. In W. Buckland (Ed.), *The film spectator: From sign to mind* (pp. 213–226). Amsterdam: Amsterdam University Press.

Odin, R. (1995b). A semio-pragmatic approach to the documentary film. In W. Buckland (Ed.), *The film spectator: From sign to mind* (pp. 227–235). Amsterdam: Amsterdam University Press.

Oosterling, H. (2000). *Radicale middelmatigheid* [Radical mediocracy]. Amsterdam: Boom.

Panhuysen, L. (2005, October 8 and 9). Het verleden laat zich niet kennen [You cannot know the past]. In *NRC Handelsblad*, p. 43.

Raessens, J. (2005). Computer games as participatory media culture. In J. Raessens & J. Goldstein (Eds.), *Handbook of computer game studies* (pp. 373–388). Cambridge, MA: MIT Press.

Renov, M. (1993a). Introduction: The truth about non-fiction. In M. Renov (Ed.), *Theorizing documentary* (pp. 1–11). New York: Routledge.

Renov, M. (1993b). Towards a poetics of documentary. In M. Renov (Ed.), *Theorizing documentary* (pp. 12–36). New York: Routledge.

Turkle, S. (1996). *Life on the screen: Identity in the age of the Internet*. London: Weidenfeld & Nicolson.

Uricchio, W. (2005). Simulation, history, and computer games. In J. Raessens & J. Goldstein (Eds.), *Handbook of computer game studies* (pp. 327–338). Cambridge, MA: MIT Press.

Winston, B. (1993). The documentary film as scientific inscription. In M. Renov (Ed.), *Theorizing documentary* (pp. 37–57). New York: Routledge.

Winston, B. (1995). *Claiming the real: The Griersonian documentary and its legitimations*. London: BFI Publishing.

POPULAR COMMUNICATION, 4(3), 225–239

The Games We Play Online and Offline: Making *Wang-tta* in Korea

Florence Chee

Simon Fraser University

This article presents an ethnographic analysis of case studies derived from fieldwork that was designed to consider the different ways Korean game players establish community online and offline. I consider ways Korean youth participate in activities at Korean computer game rooms, which can be thought of as "third places." A synthesis of the Korean concept *Wang-tta* provides extra insight into the motivations to excel at digital games and one of the strong drivers of such community membership. Korea's gaming society has many unique elements within the interplay of culture, social structure, and infrastructure.

In his work, *No sense of place: The impact of electronic media on social behavior,* Joshua Meyrowitz (1985) asserted that because of electronic media, physical location no longer matters in shaping our experiences and behaviors; nor does the physical presence of people "with" us. Although Meyrowitz concentrated primarily on television to support his analysis of electronic media, it is important to consider his work as a voice of concern over the impact of electronic media on society. Since the time of its publication, such media-centric concerns over the welfare of society have diverted much analysis to a debatably more "dangerous" and "addictive" genre of electronic media: the online videogame. My argument is that such media-centric analyses largely obscure the bigger picture of how a society responds to electronic media. Cultural artifacts such as television or videogames have different ascribed meanings depending on the cultural context. In this article, I use my case study of Korean online game communities to show how consideration of the physical location of a technology does indeed matter, and how media use differs from one culture to another.

Correspondence should be addressed to Florence Chee, School of Communication, Simon Fraser University, 515 West Hastings Street, Vancouver, British Columbia, Canada V6B 5K3. E-mail: florence.chee@gmail.com

This article reports on ethnographic fieldwork analyzing the intricate relation between the sociocultural factors at work in Korean game communities and the context in which games have become integrated into everyday life in South Korea. The nation is a world leader in broadband penetration rates, with 11.19 million broadband Internet subscribers (KGDI, 2004). Korea also boasts over 25 million resident online game players (KGDI, 2004), comprising about 54% of the population (Jamieson, 2005). The reasons for this phenomenon are the cause of much speculation at the industrial, academic, and governmental levels, especially from the $13 billion (per year) global videogames industry (Jamieson, 2005). Gamers in Korea have repeatedly made world headlines, with articles citing widespread videogame addictions, how real life social activities apparently suffer due to addictions to game parlors known as "PC [personal computer] bangs" (pronounced "bahngs" and, literally translated, meaning "PC rooms"), and even cases of online game-related deaths. Are these extreme stories of death and virtual mayhem (Gluck, 2002; Ho, 2005; Kim, 2005) the only possible accounts of Korean gaming phenomena by which the rest of the world should base their perceptions? As the media frames the problem of "online addiction," the phenomenon exists and is getting worse by the second. However, if we are to believe in the dominant diagnosis–treatment models and strategies that treat such allegedly addicted players, why then have they been largely unsuccessful in obtaining favorable results? What is the real issue at hand, if the stories of a minority of destructive gamers manage to eclipse those of the majority of gamers who are able to lead full and productive lives? To answer this question, I suggest that an in-depth look at culture, social structure, and broadband infrastructure might cast Korea's reputation for excessive online gaming in a different light and yield alternative explanations. To this effect, the objective of my ethnographic research is to dig deep, beyond existing statistics and assumptions, into Korean life to provide more cultural context and possible reasons why gaming communities are particularly compelling in Korea. Following that, one may make educated guesses as to why they are not as compelling in other parts of the world.

In *The Real World of Technology*, Ursula Franklin (1999) emphasized that technologies are developed and used within a particular social, economic, and political context. My work continues to emphasize the importance of assessing the culture in which media is created and the context in which it is used. I wish to add to the current knowledge of the interplay between technology and the development of human relationships as expressed in digital games, which are becoming increasingly recognized as a growing pastime and mode of social expression. Brian Sutton-Smith (1997), in his influential book on play theory, *The Ambiguity of Play*, asserted that the rhetorics of a larger culture will have its own socializing influence, and the norms and hierarchies of the gaming society and general society will interpenetrate the game with its own particular social arrangements. He wrote, "Playing games for the sake of games is always playing games for the sake of games in a particular social context with its own particular social arrangements. There is no lasting social play without play culture." (p. 120). In other words, to assess the longevity and sustainability of social play, it is important to look at the specific context and historical circumstances of the culture in which that play is situated.

Contrary to general media portrayal and popular belief, I argue that a relatively elevated level of gaming in Korea is not due to the game itself. The assertion that a game is particularly addictive does not address the evidence I found in the fieldwork, which points to many reasons that have little or nothing to do with the game or its genre. I found that a whole host of factors external to the game itself, such as the PC bang in which it is played, have an active role in the promotion and popular play of "old" games such as *StarCraft* (Blizzard Entertainment)—a game that came out in 1998 and has lost (or never had) in North America the renowned popularity that it still enjoys in Korea.[1] Korea's unique history, limited geographical area, and governmental support have encouraged the development of a sophisticated broadband infrastructure. The availability of broadband access in Korea has facilitated the proliferation of PC bangs. Due to their large numbers, PC bangs are highly competitive and cheaper than any other activity. Youth, with their limited incomes, often choose the PC bang as a place to commune, fulfilling the role of a "third place" (Oldenburg, 1997), as I later explain.

After painting a comprehensive picture of the cultural milieu in which gaming exists in Korea, I provide a synthesis of the Korean social issue of *Wang-tta*, which includes the act of singling out one person in a group to bully and ostracize. The issue is not commonly known or written about outside of Korea. I look at how the concept of *Wang-tta* was contrasted with admiration for people who can game excessively (and as a result, game well). I then posit the creation of *Wang-tta* as one of the motivations to excel at digital games and as a strong driver of such community membership.

As the results of this case study on Korea indicate, there is no one single cause of excessive online gaming; nor are the reasons for it a universal, cross-cultural, physical "condition" diagnosable in biomedical terms. I report and use some of the findings of this ethnography in Korea to argue that elevated participation in a gaming environment has just as much, if not more, to do with the cultural and geographical life context than the actual game itself.

METHODOLOGY AND RATIONALE

In this section, I discuss the methodology and resulting strategies I used to obtain the data used in this study. The field research for this study was conducted during a

---

[1] In Chee (2005), I discussed how other factors such as television broadcasts of professional game tournaments and industry sponsorship also play a role in the continuation of enthusiasm for a particular game.

4-month period in the fall of 2004, in Seoul, South Korea. Short-term observation was also conducted in regional centers, such as Chuncheon, Sokcho, and Cheongju.

The personal narratives of online game players in Korea were of particular interest to me. I wished to observe and analyze patterns of behavior and common histories to find out what was so compelling about these games–communities that players would supposedly conform to media stereotypes and forsake almost everything else in their lives to participate.

For this study, as described in *The Ethnographer's Method* by A. Stewart (1998), I used the "multiple modes of data collection" (p. 28) principle to compare between field data derived via different methods, which included:

- *Participant observation* for the duration of 4 months: This experience was comprised of informal information gathering from individuals and groups, and general self-immersion in cultural contexts and technological experience. The participant observation was further intensified by the home stay (which I describe next) that provided much of the cultural, linguistic, and lifestyle immersion that informs this study.
- A total of 21 *formal in-depth interviews* with gamers: These were individuals who were defined by others or self-identified as "addicted to games" in the present or past.
- Seventeen *formal online interviews*: These were conducted with gamers, some of whom also worked in the Korean gaming industry.
- Two *focus groups*: One was with 8 participants and the other was with 7 participants with mixed ages and proficiency with Internet use.

Instead of relying on just one method, I chose to rely on a number of ways to gather data. The pilot nature of this study gave me the freedom to be holistic in methodology and to choose to drill down into the themes that proved more interesting for present and future studies. For example, I could check out various assertions made by my interviewees against what I observed them or others doing during my direct observations over an extended time period. My focus group data assisted in giving me a framework with which to articulate the cacophony of information I was obtaining via the other methods. Using this strategy, I could identify the overlapping trends from the greater body of data.

I briefly summarize what allowed me to do this study, the events leading up to conducting the research and methods, and my rationale while conducting the fieldwork. One year before the fieldwork began in Korea, I prepared to conduct the ethnography by learning to read and speak Korean. Being from Vancouver, Canada, this endeavor was facilitated by my exposure to a rich multicultural environment and specifically, the large number of residents originally from Korea with whom I could continue to practice. Although it is true that the greater bulk of my learning about Korean language and culture began when my plane landed in Korea (the point of going there), it was quite valuable to have gone with the existing foundation I had built while in Vancouver. Because my research was about daily life at the grassroots, I felt that it was very important to be prepared to speak Korean and blend in as much as possible. This decision ultimately impacted my study in a positive manner, as my visually Korean appearance and use of the vernacular did indeed alleviate a great portion of the stress associated with "blending in," giving me more access to everyday things. With the length of my stay, most of the people with whom I had contact acclimatized to my presence and were able to forget that I was Canadian most of the time or, in the case of more superficial encounters, did not even realize that I was. This mutual acclimatization was one of the benefits of conducting ethnography over an extended period of time.

While in Korea, I conducted participant observation within the public and private social contexts of home, school, and everything else involved in daily life. My observations ranged from the perplexing to the mundane. Gaming culture is everywhere in Korea, every day, and my observations included everything from those recorded in and around numerous PC game rooms, to what I saw looking over the shoulder of someone playing mobile phone games on Seoul's expansive subway system.

Adding to my cultural immersion, I had the privilege of doing a home stay with a multigenerational Korean family in the heart of Seoul, as well as short-term stays in other types of Korean homes outside of Seoul, ranging from the early 20th century homes to the more common dense urban high-rise buildings. By sharing these living spaces, and fully participating in the culture (almost always blending in as a resident), I was privy to many things said and unsaid. Many of my experiences inside and outside of my family context provided much subtext for the behaviors I observed during this research. Each day, whenever possible, I would make thick descriptions (Geertz, 1973) in my field notes of what I encountered. This reflexivity was important to the study as a whole, as was a hyper-awareness of my conceptual baggage (who I was, what my assumptions were, and what I was encountering). As a woman in my mid-20s living in an urban high-rise three-generation home, I had to deal with the implications of being a member of the youngest generation in the household. With Confucian ideology as an overarching determinate of Korean everyday life, the emphasis on my placement in terms of seniority (or lack thereof) influenced the way I was viewed not only within the home to family members, but more to my chagrin, the general public. This situation enabled me to experience firsthand what it was like to navigate everyday life as a Korean youth, analyze it, reflect on it, and write about it.

I was interested in the specific stories of people navigating through their lives and their specific encounters. Being rather new to town, I had to rely on the occurrence of organized accidents to meet people.[2] The nature of this research enabled me to conduct interviews by using what is commonly known as the "snowball sampling" technique or "accidental–convenience sampling" (Richards, 1998, p. 37). The interviews took place in numerous locations and, coupled with participant observation, personal narratives provided insights into the lives of game players and their motivations for engaging in communities associated with game playing. In addition to the informal interviews that took place during my stay in Korea, I conducted formal in-depth interviews in both Korean and English with players who participated in game communities and subject matter experts in the field. Thus, the methods by and large reflect the way things are generally done in Korea—through a myriad of social networks and snowball samples. I was able to analyze friendship networks within the gamer communities and evaluate general lifestyles.

Furthermore, I conducted focus groups in which I gave participants examples of news articles about Internet addiction in South Korea and asked them to comment on the veracity of the situation as they perceived it. The varying perspectives in these focus groups were checked against the interview–participant observation data to compare the many perspectives on Internet use in Korea while gaining information about how Koreans perceive their own relations to games, the Internet, technologies, one another, and the international community at large. I found these data to be quite interesting because I was able to get the perspectives of people who had a greater variance in age and professional status, and who did not necessarily affiliate themselves with any game community.

Finally, the amount I immersed myself in Korean culture and lifestyle played a significant part in generating the research insights in this study. This immersion allowed me to more fully understand some key aspects of Korean homes. During my stay, it became apparent to me why certain behaviors encouraged or discouraged the use of certain technologies. I could understand the context in which technology and resulting gaming habits so popular among contemporary Korean youth existed, because I was living it. This participation in culture and lived experiences helped me to see the interplay of relationships both online and offline.

THE IMPORTANCE OF PC BANGS AS "THIRD PLACES" IN KOREA

According to Oldenburg (1997), *third places* are those that are neither work nor home, but are places of psychological comfort and support. These places often contain people of like mind and like interests. In Korea, such third places become

---

[2]Almost everything in Korea is done by introduction. How I exactly managed to get these introductions to do this type of research and gain rapport with my informants is an interesting story worthy of its own article, but beyond the scope of this one.

especially important because entertaining one's friends is rarely done in the home. At a third place, such as a PC bang, one can choose from online games, e-mail, online chat, Web surfing, visiting matchmaking sites, people watching, eating, smoking, being with big groups of friends, or just being with one's significant other in a friendlier setting. A PC bang also has been known to be a cheap place for shelter in the middle of the night, or within the broader context of an unkind job market, a place for the unemployed to spend the day. Given these social dynamics, the PC bang is the site of numerous significant social interactions. In my discussion of the importance of the PC bang in the lives of Korean youth, I would argue that the online games are more of a "fourth place," situated within the third places of PC bangs. The games are often not the prime motivator for people to go to a PC bang. Using what Feenberg and Bakardjieva (2004) asserted in their work on the online community as an "imaginary" social construct, I would say that these people in the PC bang are in that process of creating a community online, but they are also partaking in physical community.

The PC bang is ubiquitous in Korean everyday life. From the city street, one often sees neon signs stating the fact that the building has a PC game room or two, but they rarely exist on the first floor in which there are typically other businesses such as service shops. To find a PC bang, one must often venture up or down tiny, dingy, often dodgy looking stairs and pass through a tinted glass door. These rooms, often thick with cigarette smoke, vary in size, anywhere from 5 to 50 or more computer stations, each with its own comfortable executive chair. If the PC bang is big enough, it may have a special "couple zone" in which the stations are two computers in front of a "couple chair" (a loveseat or expanded chair without a separating armrest) made for two people to get physically closer. There may be a snack bar, varying in size with foodstuffs available. Standard items available tend to be quick snacks such as vitamin drinks, water, soft drinks, bags of chips, cookies, and instant noodle soup bowls (*ramyun*). On entry, one can get a plastic card from the clerk at the front counter. The card will have a number on it that, when entered into the greeting interface of the computer, will activate the billing time for that computer station. The rate is often about $1.00 (U.S.) per hour, with some places offering discounts at nonpeak times.[3] This rate is much more affordable to young people on a limited income than that of other, more expensive "bangs," such as "*norae bangs*" (karaoke room), "DVD bangs" (movie watching room), or board game bangs. On leaving, the clerk punches in the number of the card, and the tab is paid. PC bangs are typically very popular as places to go because of their cheap rates and are popular as startup businesses. Every neighborhood in Seoul averages about one

---

[3]It is interesting to note that the rate for PC bangs was substantially more expensive (about $10.00 U.S.) in the late 1990s. As availability and competition in PC bangs has increased, prices have decreased.

PC bang per block. They are generally open 24 hr a day, 7 days a week, and ones with newer computers are often completely full at all hours.

According to K. Stewart (2004), "The PC bang and bang culture in Korea ... [provides] children with media use opportunities outside of their home, away from parental rules and regulations and among groups of friends, which does not often happen within the Korean homes" (p. 62). My own observations and interviews concur with this assertion. For many young Koreans, their participation in online games represents one facet of a whole community and way of life. The activities surrounding this media ecology determine how its members navigate within their vital orientations and make choices in how they take nourishment, spend money, earn money, and even partake in courtship rituals. In this section, I talk about the experiences of some young Koreans and how the PC bang fits into their life contexts.

It is easy to see how one might be alarmed by Korean youths spending their hours at PC bangs. Rather than dismiss the participants as "game addicts," however, I discuss a few examples from the formal interviews that illustrate various motives for spending a lot of time at PC game rooms that were not about the games themselves at all.

One 27-year-old university student I interviewed spent as much time outside his home as possible. After classes, he would typically go to dinner with his friends; go to a PC bang in the area; and, while there, play a combination of *Lineage* (NCSoft, 1998), *StarCraft,* and *Kart Rider* (Nexon, 1998) for about 4 hr. By the time he arrived home it would typically be midnight, at which point he would log onto his computer in his room and play for another few hours. Having access to these technologies in his own room, one might think it strange that he would pay money to play the same games. When I asked why he would play at a PC bang as opposed to home, he answered that he could smoke at PC bangs, whereas at home he could not (his parents did not like it)[4]: "The biggest reason why I go to PC bang is [it's] more comfortable than home. I play games at home at midnight because my parents are sleeping." Two major reasons he cited were his lack of "comfort"[5] in his own home and deliberate avoidance of encounters with his parents. To him, the PC bang was a way to escape the various constraints of his domestic environment.

Another man in the same age group actually talked about his lack of desire to play online games, but that he did so to be with his friends:

---

[4]Although things are changing slowly to reflect Western models of behavior, it is still quite common for young Koreans to live with their parents until they are married. In fact, it is often expected. Thus, many coping strategies, such as those talked about by informants, are rather typical attitudes of youth living with their parents.

[5]Comfort as he sees it is most likely his ability to smoke elsewhere and escape the constraints of intergenerational friction he feels living with his parents as a 27-year-old man.

S: If I have time, [I go] to play with my friends after drinking. Three times or more per week.

F: And how long do you spend there?

S: 1 to 3 hours.

F: What do you play?

S: *StarCraft.*

F: How did you learn *StarCraft*? At PC bangs or at home?

S: Just PC bangs. I want to play *StarCraft* really well, but the game is difficult for me. I want to play simple games like baseball and bowling games.

The casual player discussed here reflects the sentiments of other interviewees who were either "recovering game addicts" or who "do not play." However, even those who insisted they did not play for their own amusement reported gaming least 5 hr per week with the premise of being with others and maintaining bonds with their peer groups. In addressing play as linked with social rhetoric, Sutton-Smith (1997) wrote, "It has been shown that sometimes players play primarily to be with others" (p. 105). This seems to be reflected particularly accurately in Korean play sociality.

Another social motive I encountered was using the game atmosphere in the PC bang to engage in courtship practices. A 24-year-old university student told me she had been playing the massively multiplayer online role playing game *Ragnarok* and *Kart Rider* for about 1 year, and thought she was "addicted." During the interview the informant stated that she and her boyfriend had been dating 1½ years. After the first 6 months of their relationship, she started playing computer games with him at PC bangs.[6] When I asked about her motives for playing, our conversation went as follows:

S: This time was winter, so it was very cold outside. We could spend less money in the PC room because it was cheap compared to using other facilities.

F: Just to spend time together in a warm place?

S: Yes. We can spend time together in a warm place. I am a student, and I don't have a lot of money. So, that's a good way to spend time with my boyfriend.

---

[6]Although the fact that online game play is still male dominated in this context is intriguing, the gender implications of gaming are beyond the scope of this particular article. The common stereotype, which was reflected by the girls with whom I spoke, seems to indicate that women or girls tend to like "simple" games such as *Kart Rider* or *Tetris* (Pajitnov, 1985).

Although she said that the games she played were fun and the time she spent at PC bangs ranged from 15 to 20 hr per week, throughout the interview it was clear that her motives for going to the PC bang were not so much about the games themselves, but rather what the venue offered for nurturing her relationship with her boyfriend.

Finding the courtship and PC bang link interesting, I later interviewed a couple in their early 20s who played *Lineage* together almost 40 hr per week. Although they were helping each other cut down their *Lineage* play online, it was their mutual passion for the game that initially had allowed them to meet offline at a *Lineage* meet. He saw her, and it was "love at first sight." She, however, did not notice him and ignored his advances. After the meeting, they would encounter one another online in *Lineage,* in which he would then try to protect her from harm against enemy attacks. After a while, this impressed her enough so that she consented to having a date with him. Their relationship slowly evolved, and as of the time of the writing of this article, they are very happy, very much in love, and still going to PC bangs together.

Although Oldenburg (1997) wrote about third places for and within a U.S. context, similar parallels can be drawn for the importance of these third places in Korea. It is important to see the particular importance of PC bangs in Korean everyday life. It is significant that these places function neither as work nor home, and are places of psychological (and in this case even physical) comfort and support. It also is significant that wide use of the PC bang is due primarily to the availability and cheap price of access at $1.00 per hour. For these reasons, the PC bang has become the locus of so many varied community- nurturing activities among young Koreans.

THE "WANG-TTA," MAKING "WANG-TTA," AND "WANG-TTA" OF EVERYONE

A fascinating concept, *Wang-tta,* emerged in my interviews with Korean gamers. Put simply, in this context the term describes isolating and bullying the worst game player in one's peer group. It is a difficult term to translate into English, and very little English literature that attempts to do so exists. One can be said to either "make *Wang-tta*" or be the object of *Wang-tta.* The term is paradigmatically similar to (and some have said modeled after) the Japanese term for bullying, *Ijime.* In reference to *Ijime* situations, Dogakinai (1999) stated that in collectivist societies such as Japan, similarity is a source of comfort, whereas difference is disparaged and subject to much abuse from others.

I first came across the term in one of the formal interviews (shown next) when my informant was trying to address his motivations for playing games. My ignorance of this concept was almost amusing in retrospect:

S: Do you know *Wang-tta*?

F: Is he a pro gamer?

S: No, [it's a] social problem word. *Wang-tta* ... if one person can't play the game ... Think about it this way: Every class[room] has a little or poor ... all people hate him. If one class has 40 people, 39 people playing a game together, but 1 person can't play the game. 39 people then hate him, and he wants to play together with them but he couldn't because he can't play that well. So, after time goes, this gap is increased. So everyone hates him. Everyone hates him.

At first, I was uncertain as to whether *Wang-tta* was being used as a noun to describe the individual "loser" (as it commonly tends to be used in English) or as a verb or adverb to describe the bullying situation. I asked for clarification, and obtained a hypothesis from an insightful informant. His supposition was that a primary motivator to play games in Korea was to achieve social acceptance among peers. In my interview with him, he also hinted at the PC bang serving as an arena of talent exhibition. That is, one might practice playing at home to "perform" at the PC bang where his or her talents in a game would then be scrutinized and "peer-reviewed." Sitting across a table from me, he drew a diagram of many people in a circle, and lines representing negativity between those people and one isolated person away from the main circle. I asked for clarification:

F: So this one is the *Wang-tta*. The outlier is the *Wang-tta*.

S: The *whole situation* is *Wang-tta* <circling the whole diagram>. People say he is *Wang-tta* <pointing to the isolated person in the diagram>. If someone can't play the game ... that situation makes this <diagram> situation sometimes. So everyone doesn't want to be *Wang-tta*. *That is why many people play games in Korea.* Everyone likes a person who can play the game very well. That's why every day students practice games at home.

Thankfully, I was at an early point in my study in which I could ask more informants about the concept of *Wang-tta*. The concept was intriguing enough to follow up on for subsequent interviews. As I had built flexibility into my interview protocol, I was able to quickly adapt this and other new findings as I went along.

Refusal to partake in game play could subject one to isolation and ridicule. The fear of being made a "*Wang-tta*" could indeed cause many young people take every opportunity to practice the games of their peer groups to become more skilled and less subject to such ridicule. A person who possesses a social deficit, articulated by others as *Wang-tta,* could develop in many situations in which there is immense social pressure to be good at games. Johan Huizinga's (1955) discussion of the way spoilsports are treated is comparable to the creation of *Wang-tta*: "The player who trespasses against the rules or ignores them is a 'spoil-sport' ... Therefore he must be cast out for he threatens the existence of the play-community" (p. 11). Caillois (1961) concurred with Huizinga in that, "the game is ruined by the nihilist who denounces the rules as absurd and conventional, who refuses to play because the game is meaningless" (p. 7). In threatening the sanctity of the play community, one might subject oneself to being singled out as *Wang-tta*.

Here is another person's concept of *Wang-tta*:

F: Can you tell me what your definition of *Wang-tta* is?

S: *Wang-tta* is [a] bad thing. Everyone doesn't like a *Wang-tta*. They have a different mind, different behavior. So when one guy doesn't like another guy... *Wang-tta* is some group, and one guy is made the weirdo.

It is important to note that in the concept of *Wang-tta* there is fusion between collectivism and individualism, in that one's talent might not be the only consideration for prevention of ostracization.

The *Wang-tta* Effect

In my quest for the elusive *Wang-tta*, I came across what I call the *Wang-tta effect*, which describes what I see as a retreat of one player from the given community due to a circumstance beyond the would-be player's control. Such circumstances often include a once-frequent game player being removed from one's peer group for an extended period of time, for example, while serving in the army for 2 years or going abroad to learn English for 1 year or more. Once such a player returns back to the home community, game play time has typically dropped significantly. Implicit in informant's statements such as, "it's no longer fun" or "my priorities changed," I see the *Wang-tta* effect occurring due to the informant's unwillingness to subject themselves to *Wang-tta* from their peer group. The examples I discuss next show how culture (in this case *Wang-tta*), social structure, and infrastructure interact to influence player motives and habits.

For example, in one interview, I spoke to a 25-year-old man in his final year of university. At first, he claimed that he no longer played online games, but as the interview went on, this proved to not be the case.

F: How long have you been gaming?

S: Seven years, maybe. Since I was 20. I stopped for maybe 2½ years, because I was addicted to *Starcraft*. For 4 years, I played *StarCraft* a lot. After I quit the army, I recognized that I was really bad at playing *StarCraft*. Because after that everyone played *StarCraft* really well, but not me. So before I went to the army I was kind of a regular player, but after I quit from the army, *I was the lower class player.* So I just quit because I wasn't very good at *StarCraft.*

I knew from my observation that this individual spent time at PC bangs, had social gatherings centering with game tournaments, and other such activities. This left me wondering, so I asked for clarification.

F: So when you go to a PC bang, is it only for friends?

S: Yes, mostly. I go to PC room with my friends to play games with my friends. But if I go just by myself it's not fun. I'm not good at games, but if I go to a PC bang with my friends, we can make a team and play with other teams. So it's kind of socialization. So I like that. Not playing by myself. Before we went to the army, we played *StarCraft* all the time together. When I was in the army, I was dying to go online. I wanted to play *StarCraft,* but I couldn't. They didn't allow it. After I quit from the army, of course I played *StarCraft,* but it wasn't very much fun compared to before the army. I was defeated by people.

F: Ok, now I don't know very much about army service here. When people are doing military service, they don't do school or anything else?

S: We stayed at the army base 2 years and 2 months. We could only go out 45 days. That is the only vacation we have. Four or five times. Ten days. Ten days per vacation. During the army service, we cannot go out. Even though we go outside, we cannot do things like drink alcohol, or play games.

Clearly, there are issues in the social structure unique in many ways to Korean life. Among young Korean men, military service functions as both training and, more significantly in a social manner, a rite of passage that signals a clear demarcation between one's relatively carefree youth and responsible, career-oriented adulthood. The typical severing of social networks during this time of military service also has much to do with ambivalent feelings of how one will be received back into the social network of origin.

Yet another example of the *Wang-tta* effect can be seen in the story of an extremely hardcore game player (he has repeatedly engaged in 36-hr-long tournaments) who was cut off from most of his peer group as well as Korea's broadband infrastructure when he went to England to study English.

F: How much time do you spend per week playing games?

S: Nowadays 6 to 7 hours per week because this is my last semester [at university]. So, I'm really busy. I have to study harder than [ever] before for getting a job. The biggest reason [for cutting back on gaming] is studying because it's my last semester.

F: At the time you spent 36 hours playing, when did you start cutting down?

S: During my stay in England. That was a big reason. Their Internet speed is much slower. Very slow. I couldn't play a game [online] for nearly 1 year. So that's why. After that, I lost my temper. I lost interest in playing games.

F: Because you were doing other things?

S: Yeah I couldn't play games... Still, my friends played games, so [after I got back] I restarted with them.

When I asked what he ended up doing in England instead of playing online games, with a chuckle he responded, "Drinking. Smoking."

The concept of the *Wang-tta* effect illustrates the often implicit concern over a lack of ability to participate in online game activities in peer groups after an absence. It also seemed important to be able to participate well after investing a lot of practice time.[7] In my encounters with Korean gamers, in interviews and focus groups, the ability to do something "extremely well," in the areas of school or games, is very much taken seriously and admired.

CONCLUSION: UNDERSTANDING KOREAN EXPERIENCES

Throughout this article, I suggest that an in-depth look at culture, social structure, and infrastructure might cast Korea's reputation for excessive online gaming in a different light. By engaging in this first-hand, multimethod, ethnographic study, I hoped to provide more cultural context and possible explanations for why gaming and its associated activities seem so immersive and compelling in Korea. In addition to that, one may make educated guesses as to why they are not as compelling in other parts of the world. The original fieldwork concerning the PC bang as a third place, merged with theories of play, add perspective to game research by highlighting the concept of online sociability as it is created in the interactions between players, online and offline.

---

[7]I identified the *Wang-tta* effect with young Korean men, but at this time am uncertain of an equivalent with women in gaming. There are definitely gender differences in the way women as opposed to men are esteemed in their peer groups. My data indicate that women's skill in gaming was not perceived as important.

Moreover the Korean social phenomenon of *Wang-tta,* which includes the act of singling out one person in a group to bully and treat as an outcast provides additional insight into one of the motivations to excel at digital games and one of the strong drivers of such community membership. As the results of this case study on Korea indicate, the factors for excessive online gaming are most likely not cross-cultural (i.e., diagnosable as addiction in biomedical terms) and just as likely, if not more, to do with the offline "game" of one's life context. In this case study, the offline *place* of Korea, as well as a "sense of place" for Korean youth was integral in understanding the many complexities inherent in the way Korean online game culture has come to be in its current state of being.

REFERENCES

Blizzard Entertainment. (1998). StarCraft. [Computer software]. Irvine, CA: Author.

Caillois, R. (1961). *Man, play, and games.* New York: Free Press.

Chee, F. (2005). *Essays on korean online game communities.* Unpublished masters thesis, Simon Fraser University, Burnaby.

Dogakinai, A. (1999). *Ijime: A social illness of Japan.* Retrieved January 09, 2005, from http://www.lclark.edu/~krauss/advwrf99/causeeffect/akikocause.html

Feenberg, A., & Bakardjieva, M. (2004). Virtual community: No "killer implication." *New Media & Society, 6*(1), 37–43.

Franklin, U. (1999). *The real world of technology.* Toronto, Canada: Anansi.

Geertz, C. (1973). *The interpretation of cultures: Selected essays.* New York: Basic Books.

Gluck, C. (2002). *South Korea's gaming addicts.* Retrieved June 30, 2003, from http://news.bbc.co.uk/1/hi/world/asia- pacific/2499957.stm

Gravity Corp. (2002). Ragnarok Online. [Computer software]. Seoul, Korea: Author.

Ho, A. (2005, March 18). Broadband: Virtually a den of iniquity? *The Straits Times,* p. 27.

Huizinga, J. (1955). *Homo ludens: A study of the play element in culture.* Boston: Beacon.

Jamieson, J. (2005, May 22). Video gaming holds Korea in its grip. *The Province,* p. A41.

Korea Game Development Institute. (2004). Comparison of the characteristics of gamers in Korea and Japan. *Journal of Game Industry and Culture, 5,* 18.

Kim, T. (2005). *Internet addiction haunts Korea.* Retrieved January 21, 2005, from http://search.hankooki.com/times/times_view.php?terms=Internet+haunts+Korea+code%3A+kt&path=hankooki3%2Ftimes%2Flpage%2F200501%2Fkt200501211746495346 0.htm&kw=Internet%20haunts%20Korea

Meyrowitz, J. (1985). *No sense of place: The impact of electronic media on social behavior.* New York: Oxford University Press.

Nexon. (1998). Kart Rider. [Computer software]. Santa Clara, CA: Author.

Oldenburg, R. (1997). *The great good place.* New York: Marlowe and Company.

Pajitnov, A. (1985). Tetris. [Computer software]. Various.

Richards, W. (1998). *The Zen of empirical research.* Creskill, NJ: Hampton.

Song, J. (1998). Lineage. [Computer software]. Seoul, Korea: NCSoft.

Stewart, A. (1998). *The ethnographer's method* (Vol. 46). Thousand Oaks, CA: Sage.

Stewart, K. (2004). *Informatization of a nation: A case study of South Korea's computer gaming and PC-Bang culture.* Unpublished masters thesis, Simon Fraser University, Burnaby, British Columbia, Canada.

Sutton-Smith, B. (1997). *The ambiguity of play.* Cambridge, MA: Harvard University Press.